PostgreSQL
100 Interview Questions

X.Y. Wang

Contents

1 Introduction   **13**

2 Basic   **15**

   2.1   What is PostgreSQL and why is it popular? 15

   2.2   Can you explain the difference between SQL and Post-
        greSQL? 16

   2.3   What is the role of a database in a web application,
        and why would you choose PostgreSQL for your project? 17

   2.4   What is the difference between primary key, foreign
        key, and unique key in PostgreSQL? 19

   2.5   What is a schema in PostgreSQL and what is its pur-
        pose? 21

   2.6   What are the basic data types available in PostgreSQL? 21

   2.7   How do you create a new database and user in Post-
        greSQL? 23

   2.8   How do you connect to a PostgreSQL database using
        a command-line interface (CLI)? 24

   2.9   What is the purpose of an index in PostgreSQL and
        when should you use it? 26

2.10 What is a transaction and how does PostgreSQL han-
      dle transactions?   27

2.11 Can you explain the difference between DDL, DML,
      and DCL in PostgreSQL?   28

2.12 What are the different types of joins in PostgreSQL,
      and how do they work?   30

2.13 What are the aggregate functions available in Post-
      greSQL, and what are their purposes?   32

2.14 How do you implement pagination in PostgreSQL to
      display a limited number of rows per page?   34

2.15 What is the difference between a view and a table in
      PostgreSQL, and when should you use each one? . . .   35

2.16 How do you perform a basic SELECT query in Post-
      greSQL, including filtering, sorting, and limiting results? 36

2.17 What is the purpose of the WHERE clause in Post-
      greSQL, and how does it work?   37

2.18 Can you explain the difference between GROUP BY
      and ORDER BY in PostgreSQL?   38

2.19 How do you create and use stored procedures and
      functions in PostgreSQL?   40

2.20 What are triggers in PostgreSQL, and what are some
      common use cases for them?   41

3 Intermediate   **45**

3.1   What is the ACID property in databases, and how
      does PostgreSQL ensure ACID compliance?   45

3.2   Explain the concept of MVCC (Multi-Version Con-
      currency Control) in PostgreSQL and how it affects
      transaction isolation.   47

3.3   What is the difference between the VACUUM and AN-
       ALYZE operations in PostgreSQL, and when should
       you use them?   48

3.4   How do you perform a backup and restore of a Post-
       greSQL database using pg_dump and pg_restore? . .   49

3.5   Explain the role of the Write-Ahead Log (WAL) in
       PostgreSQL and how it contributes to data durability.   51

3.6   How do you create and manage database indexes in
       PostgreSQL to optimize query performance?   52

3.7   What are the different types of locking mechanisms in
       PostgreSQL and how do they work?   54

3.8   Explain the concept of prepared statements in Post-
       greSQL and their benefits.   56

3.9   What is the difference between UNION, UNION ALL,
       INTERSECT, and EXCEPT operations in PostgreSQL?   57

3.10 How do you set up and manage replication in Post-
       greSQL for high availability and load balancing? . . .   60

3.11 What are the different types of constraints in Post-
       greSQL, and how do they help maintain data integrity?   62

3.12 How do you use the EXPLAIN and EXPLAIN AN-
       ALYZE commands to analyze query performance in
       PostgreSQL?   65

3.13 What is the difference between a full-text search and a
       LIKE query in PostgreSQL, and when should you use
       each?   66

3.14 How do you work with arrays and JSON data types
       in PostgreSQL?   67

3.15 What are some performance tuning techniques you can
       apply to optimize PostgreSQL database performance?   69

3.16 How do you manage user roles and permissions in
       PostgreSQL?   71

3.17 Explain the concept of table partitioning in Post-
      greSQL and its benefits.   72

3.18 What are some common database maintenance tasks
      that a PostgreSQL DBA should perform?   74

3.19 How do you use window functions in PostgreSQL, and
      what are their advantages?   75

3.20 What is the purpose of the .pgpass file, and how do
      you use it to securely store PostgreSQL passwords? . .   76

4 Advanced   79

4.1 What are the different types of indexes in PostgreSQL,
      and when should you use each one?   79

4.2 Explain the role of the Query Planner and Query Op-
      timizer in PostgreSQL's internal workings.   81

4.3 How do you monitor and manage the performance of
      PostgreSQL using tools like pg_stat_statements and
      pgBadger?   82

4.4 Describe the process of setting up and configuring
      connection pooling in PostgreSQL using tools like Pg-
      Bouncer or Pgpool-II.   84

4.5 Explain the role of tablespaces in PostgreSQL and how
      they can be used for disk space management.   85

4.6 How do you perform point-in-time recovery (PITR) in
      PostgreSQL using WAL archives and base backups? .   86

4.7 What are the different isolation levels in PostgreSQL,
      and how do they affect transaction behavior and per-
      formance?   88

4.8 Explain the concept of full-text search in PostgreSQL,
      including text search functions, text search operators,
      and tsvector and tsquery data types.   89

4.9   How do you manage database schema migrations in PostgreSQL using tools like Flyway or Sqitch?   91

4.10   How do you use foreign data wrappers (FDWs) in PostgreSQL to query data from external sources like other databases or CSV files?   93

4.11   What are the various options for sharding in PostgreSQL, and what are their trade-offs?   95

4.12   How do you use logical replication in PostgreSQL to replicate specific tables or schemas between databases?   96

4.13   What are some techniques to troubleshoot and resolve deadlocks in PostgreSQL?   98

4.14   Describe the role of the autovacuum process in PostgreSQL and how it affects performance and storage. .   100

4.15   What is the concept of savepoints in PostgreSQL, and how can they be used in transaction management? . .   101

4.16   How do you handle large objects (LOBs) in PostgreSQL, including BLOBs and CLOBs?   102

4.17   How do you use the NOTIFY and LISTEN features in PostgreSQL to implement publish-subscribe patterns?   104

4.18   Explain the difference between the Serializable and Snapshot Isolation levels in PostgreSQL, and their implications on transaction management.   106

4.19   What are the various approaches for migrating data between PostgreSQL instances, such as logical backups, physical backups, and replication?   108

4.20   How do you implement and manage high availability and failover solutions in PostgreSQL using tools like repmgr or Patroni?   110

5   Expert   113

5.1   Describe PostgreSQL's internal architecture, including components like the parser, the planner/optimizer, and the executor. 113

5.2   Explain how PostgreSQL uses write-ahead logging (WAL) for crash recovery and replication, and how it affects database performance. 115

5.3   How do you implement advanced monitoring and alerting for PostgreSQL using tools like Grafana, Prometheus, and Zabbix? 116

5.4   Describe the process of tuning PostgreSQL's configuration settings, such as shared_buffers, work_mem, and maintenance_work_mem, for optimal performance. 118

5.5   How do you manage schema changes in a zero-downtime environment for PostgreSQL? 120

5.6   Explain the concept of just-in-time (JIT) compilation in PostgreSQL and how it can improve query performance. 122

5.7   How do you use materialized views in PostgreSQL for complex query optimization and data warehousing scenarios? 123

5.8   What are some advanced techniques for optimizing complex SQL queries in PostgreSQL, such as query refactoring, indexing strategies, and partitioning? . . . 125

5.9   Discuss the implications of using different storage engines and filesystems with PostgreSQL, such as ZFS, XFS, and EXT4. 127

5.10 Describe the challenges and best practices for scaling PostgreSQL horizontally using sharding or partitioning solutions like Citus or PL/Proxy. 130

5.11 How do you implement advanced security features in PostgreSQL, such as transparent data encryption (TDE), data masking, and row-level security? 132

5.12 Explain the concept of two-phase commit (2PC) in PostgreSQL and its role in distributed transactions. . 134

5.13 How do you optimize PostgreSQL's performance for geospatial data and queries using the PostGIS extension? 136

5.14 Describe the process of upgrading PostgreSQL to a newer version, including major version upgrades and the challenges involved. 137

5.15 What are some best practices for disaster recovery planning in a PostgreSQL environment? 139

5.16 Explain the role of consistency checks and validation in PostgreSQL, including tools like pg_checksums and pg_repack. 140

5.17 How do you integrate PostgreSQL with big data and data warehousing solutions, such as Hadoop, Apache Spark, or Amazon Redshift? 141

5.18 Discuss the challenges and techniques for optimizing PostgreSQL's performance in a cloud environment, such as AWS RDS, Google Cloud SQL, or Azure Database for PostgreSQL. 143

5.19 How do you manage and optimize PostgreSQL in a containerized environment using technologies like Docker and Kubernetes? 145

5.20 Describe the process of implementing advanced backup and recovery strategies in PostgreSQL, such as incremental backups, parallel backups, and synthetic backups. 147

6 Guru **149**

6.1 Discuss the process of contributing to the PostgreSQL open-source project, including the PostgreSQL community, mailing lists, and the patch submission and review process. 149

6.2   Explain how PostgreSQL's query planner utilizes statis-
       tics and histograms for query optimization and how to
       influence its behavior.   151

6.3   Describe the internals of PostgreSQL's indexing mech-
       anisms, including B-trees, GiST, SP-GiST, GIN, and
       RUM indexes, and their use cases.   152

6.4   How do you diagnose and resolve performance bot-
       tlenecks in PostgreSQL using advanced profiling and
       diagnostic tools, such as perf, gdb, and DTrace?   154

6.5   Discuss the process of benchmarking and stress-testing
       PostgreSQL deployments using tools like pgbench, sys-
       bench, and TPC-C/TPC-H benchmarks.   155

6.6   Explain the internals of PostgreSQL's concurrency
       control mechanisms, including lock management, dead-
       locks, and lock escalation.   158

6.7   Describe the architecture of PostgreSQL's streaming
       replication and how it can be extended or customized
       for specific use cases.   160

6.8   Discuss the process of designing and implementing cus-
       tom PostgreSQL extensions, including new data types,
       operators, and functions.   162

6.9   How do you integrate PostgreSQL with machine learn-
       ing and AI solutions, such as TensorFlow, PyTorch, or
       scikit-learn, for advanced data analysis?   164

6.10   Explain the role of query parallelism in PostgreSQL
       and how it can be fine-tuned for different workloads
       and hardware configurations.   166

6.11   Describe the internals of PostgreSQL's transaction log,
       including log truncation, log shipping, and checkpointing. 168

6.12   Discuss the challenges and solutions for PostgreSQL
       deployments in hybrid or multi-cloud environments, in-
       cluding data synchronization and latency concerns. . .   170

6.13 How do you design and implement advanced sharding and partitioning schemes in PostgreSQL to handle
massive amounts of data and complex workloads? . . . 171

6.14 Explain the internals of PostgreSQL's recovery and
crash-consistency mechanisms, including checkpointing, redo, and undo. 173

6.15 Discuss the process of developing custom foreign data
wrappers (FDWs) for PostgreSQL to integrate with
new data sources or APIs. 175

6.16 Describe the principles of geographically distributed
PostgreSQL deployments, including data replication,
consistency, and latency concerns. 177

6.17 How do you implement real-time analytics and stream
processing in PostgreSQL using extensions like
TimescaleDB and PipelineDB? 179

6.18 Discuss the challenges and best practices for migrating
large-scale legacy databases to PostgreSQL, including
schema conversion, data migration, and performance
tuning. 181

6.19 Explain the internals of PostgreSQL's memory management and caching mechanisms, such as the buffer
cache, shared buffers, and local caches. 183

6.20 Describe the process of diagnosing and resolving issues
related to data corruption, disk failures, and hardware
faults in a PostgreSQL environment. 184

Chapter 1

Introduction

Welcome to "PostgreSQL: 100 Interview Questions". As one of the most popular and powerful open-source relational database management systems, PostgreSQL has earned a reputation for its performance, robustness, and advanced features. With the increasing demand for PostgreSQL in various industries, it has become imperative for database professionals, developers, and administrators to gain expertise in this technology.

This book is designed to help you prepare for interviews that involve PostgreSQL, whether you're a beginner, intermediate, or advanced user. The questions and answers presented in this book cover a wide range of topics, from basic concepts and SQL queries to advanced features and optimization techniques. By working through these questions, you will not only enhance your understanding of PostgreSQL but also develop the confidence required to succeed in an interview.

The book is divided into five sections based on the level of expertise:

Basic: This section covers the fundamental concepts and basic SQL queries in PostgreSQL. It is aimed at readers who are just starting their journey with PostgreSQL and need a solid understanding of the basics.

Intermediate: This section delves deeper into PostgreSQL's features and provides a comprehensive understanding of various database op-

erations, such as indexing, transactions, and replication. It is suitable
for readers who have some experience with PostgreSQL and want to
expand their knowledge.

Advanced: In this section, we explore more complex topics, such as
performance tuning, high availability, and point-in-time recovery. It
is designed for readers who have a strong foundation in PostgreSQL
and want to gain expertise in specific areas.

Expert: This section covers advanced topics, such as PostgreSQL's
internal architecture, JIT compilation, and geospatial data handling
using PostGIS. It targets readers who have extensive experience with
PostgreSQL and want to deepen their understanding of its inner workings and advanced features.

Guru: In the final section, we discuss topics related to contributing to
the PostgreSQL open-source project, diagnosing performance bottlenecks, and implementing custom PostgreSQL extensions. This section
is meant for readers who are passionate about PostgreSQL and want
to contribute to its development or become experts in optimizing and
extending its capabilities.

Each section contains 20 carefully selected questions, and each ques-
tion is followed by a detailed explanation to ensure that you fully
understand the concepts involved. This book is designed to be a
valuable resource not only for interview preparation but also for mas-
tering PostgreSQL in your day-to-day work.

We hope that "PostgreSQL: 100 Interview Questions" will be an in-
dispensable resource for you as you advance in your career with PostgreSQL. Happy learning!

Chapter 2

Basic

2.1 What is PostgreSQL and why is it popular?

PostgreSQL is a powerful, open-source object-relational database management system (ORDBMS) that is known for its reliability, scalability, and extensibility. It was originally developed at the University of California, Berkeley in the 1980s, and has since grown to become one of the most popular database systems in the world.

PostgreSQL is popular for several reasons:

1. Open-source: PostgreSQL is open-source software, which means that anyone can use, modify, and distribute it without paying licensing fees. This has helped to make PostgreSQL a popular choice for both small and large organizations.

2. Reliability: PostgreSQL is known for its reliability and stability. It has a reputation for being one of the most robust database systems available, and is often used in critical systems where downtime is not an option.

3. Scalability: PostgreSQL is designed to be scalable, and can handle very large datasets with ease. It is an excellent choice for applications

that require high throughput and low latency.

4. Extensibility: PostgreSQL is highly extensible, and allows users to add custom data types, operators, and functions to the database. This makes it a very flexible system that can be customized to meet the needs of different applications.

5. Comprehensive SQL support: PostgreSQL supports a wide range of SQL features, including complex queries, subselects, and transactions. It also supports many advanced SQL features, such as window functions and common table expressions.

Overall, PostgreSQL is popular because it is a powerful, flexible, and reliable database system that can be used for a wide range of applications. Its open-source nature also means that it has a large and active community of developers and users who are constantly working to improve the system and add new features.

2.2   Can you explain the difference between SQL and PostgreSQL?

SQL, or Structured Query Language, is a standard programming language used for database management and manipulation. It is a language that can be implemented across many different database management systems, including PostgreSQL. PostgreSQL, on the other hand, is a specific relational database management system that uses SQL as its primary language.

PostgreSQL is an open-source RDBMS that has advanced features such as object-relational mapping (ORM), JSON support, and full-text search, which are not present in other database systems. PostgreSQL has a strong focus on data integrity and is known for its reliability, performance, and scalability.

In terms of syntax, PostgreSQL is fully compliant with the SQL standard and includes some additional features specific to PostgreSQL. For example, PostgreSQL allows users to create custom data types and uses a rich set of functions to manipulate data.

Here is an example of creating a table with some sample data in

PostgreSQL using SQL:

```
CREATE TABLE employees (
  id serial PRIMARY KEY,
  name varchar(50),
  age integer,
  salary numeric(10,2)
);

INSERT INTO employees (name, age, salary)
VALUES ('John␣Doe', 30, 60000.00),
       ('Jane␣Smith', 25, 50000.00),
       ('Bob␣Johnson', 50, 75000.00);
```

This SQL code creates a new table named "employees" with columns for "id", "name", "age", and "salary". It then inserts three rows of sample data into the table.

In summary, SQL is a language used for database management and manipulation, while PostgreSQL is a specific RDBMS that uses SQL as its primary language and has advanced features that set it apart from other database systems.

2.3 What is the role of a database in a web application, and why would you choose PostgreSQL for your project?

The database plays a critical role in web applications by providing a structured and organized repository for storing, retrieving, and managing data. In a web application, the database typically stores user information, product information, and any other persistent data required by the application.

PostgreSQL is a popular choice for web applications because of its robustness, scalability, and rich features. Here are some reasons why you might choose PostgreSQL for your project:

1. ACID compliance: PostgreSQL is fully ACID-compliant, which means that your data is guaranteed to be consistent, durable, and free from any data integrity issues.

2. Scalability: PostgreSQL is capable of handling large amounts of

data and complex queries while ensuring high performance and availability.

3. Extensibility: PostgreSQL provides a flexible architecture that
allows you to customize your database to your specific needs. It also
supports a wide range of programming languages, including Java,
which makes it an ideal choice for web applications.

4. Security: PostgreSQL provides advanced security features such
as robust authentication and authorization mechanisms, SSL encryption, and support for multiple authentication methods.

5. Open-source: PostgreSQL is an open-source database, which means
you can use it for free and modify the source code to suit your needs.

Here's an example Java code that demonstrates how to connect to a
PostgreSQL database and execute a query:

```java
import java.sql.*;

public class PostgreSQLExample {
    public static void main(String[] args) {
        Connection conn = null;
        PreparedStatement stmt = null;
        ResultSet rs = null;

        try {
            // Register the PostgreSQL driver
            Class.forName("org.postgresql.Driver");

            // Connect to the database
            conn = DriverManager.getConnection("jdbc:postgresql://localhost/
                mydatabase", "myuser", "mypassword");

            // Execute a query
            stmt = conn.prepareStatement("SELECT * FROM users WHERE id = ?");
            stmt.setInt(1, 1);
            rs = stmt.executeQuery();

            // Process the results
            while (rs.next()) {
                System.out.println(rs.getString("firstname") + " " + rs.getString("
                    lastname"));
            }
        } catch (Exception e) {
            e.printStackTrace();
        } finally {
            try { rs.close(); } catch (Exception e) { /* ignored */ }
            try { stmt.close(); } catch (Exception e) { /* ignored */ }
            try { conn.close(); } catch (Exception e) { /* ignored */ }
        }
    }
}
```

This code connects to a PostgreSQL database, executes a query to
retrieve a user by ID, and then outputs their first and last names to

the console.

2.4   What is the difference between primary key, foreign key, and unique key in PostgreSQL?

In PostgreSQL, a primary key, a foreign key and a unique key are used to enforce different types of integrity constraints on the data stored in a table.

- Primary key: A primary key is a column or a set of columns in a table that uniquely identifies each row in the table. It must have a unique value for each row, and it cannot have a NULL value. A table can have only one primary key. Primary keys are used to enforce entity integrity, which means that they ensure that each row in a table is unique and identifiable.

Example in Java:

Suppose we have a table named 'students' with columns 'id', 'name', 'age', and 'gender'. We can define the 'id' column as a primary key like this:

```
CREATE TABLE students (
    id SERIAL PRIMARY KEY,
    name VARCHAR(50),
    age INTEGER,
    gender CHAR(1)
);
```

Here, we use the 'SERIAL' data type to automatically generate a unique value for the 'id' column for each new row inserted into the table. By making 'id' the primary key, we ensure that each row in the 'students' table is unique and identifiable by its unique 'id'.

- Foreign key: A foreign key is a column or a set of columns in a table that refers to the primary key of another table. It establishes a relationship between two tables, where the values in the foreign key column(s) of one table correspond to the values in the primary key column(s) of the other table. The purpose of a foreign key is to enforce referential integrity, which means that it ensures that the data in one table is consistent with the data in another table. A table can have multiple foreign keys.

Example in Java:

Suppose we have another table named 'enrollments' with columns 'student_id', 'course_id', and 'grade'. We can define a foreign key on the 'student_id' column that references the 'id' column of the 'students' table like this:

```
CREATE TABLE enrollments (
    student_id INTEGER REFERENCES students(id),
    course_id INTEGER,
    grade VARCHAR(2)
);
```

Here, we use the 'REFERENCES' keyword to specify that the 'student_id' column references the 'id' column of the 'students' table. This foreign key ensures that the 'student_id' value in each row of the 'enrollments' table corresponds to a valid 'id' value in the 'students' table.

- Unique key: A unique key is a column or a set of columns in a table that has a unique value for each row, similar to a primary key. However, unlike primary keys, unique keys can have NULL values. A table can have multiple unique keys. Unique keys are used to enforce domain integrity, which means that they ensure that the data in a column or a set of columns is unique.

Example in Java:

Suppose we have a table named 'employees' with columns 'id', 'name', 'email', and 'phone'. We can define a unique key on the 'email' column to ensure that each email is used only once in the 'employees' table like this:

```
CREATE TABLE employees (
    id SERIAL,
    name VARCHAR(50),
    email VARCHAR(50) UNIQUE,
    phone VARCHAR(20)
);
```

Here, we use the 'UNIQUE' keyword to specify that the 'email' column must have a unique value for each row. This unique key ensures that no two employees have the same email address.

2.5   What is a schema in PostgreSQL and what is its purpose?

In PostgreSQL, a schema is a named container for database objects, such as tables, indexes, or views. A schema is a logical grouping of objects, and each schema can contain multiple objects.

The primary purpose of using schemas is to organize database objects and to provide a namespace for those objects. By providing logical groupings of objects in schemas, it becomes easier to manage large databases with hundreds or thousands of objects. Schemas also allow for easier database management for large multi-tenant systems where multiple applications run on the same database server.

Schemas help to avoid naming collisions between objects by organizing tables and other objects under a single namespace. For example, in a single database, you might have multiple applications that all require a "user" table. By creating a separate schema for each application, you can avoid naming conflicts and allow each application to have its "user" table without affecting the other applications.

Here's an example of how to create a schema in PostgreSQL using Java code:

```
try(Connection conn = DriverManager.getConnection("jdbc:postgresql://localhost
    /mydatabase", "myuser", "mypassword")) {
  Statement stmt = conn.createStatement();
  stmt.execute("CREATE SCHEMA myschema");
}
```

This Java code connects to a database named 'mydatabase' and creates a new schema called 'myschema'. Once the schema is created, you can create database objects such as tables or views within the schema.

2.6   What are the basic data types available in PostgreSQL?

PostgreSQL supports several data types, including but not limited to:

1. Numeric Data Types:

- Integer (int): a whole number of varying sizes depending on the range needed (e.g., integer, smallint, bigint)

- Floating-point numbers: values with decimal points with varying ranges and precisions (e.g., float, decimal, numeric)

- Serial: a type of integer that automatically increments as values are added to a column

2. Character Data Types:

- Char (character): a fixed-length string of characters

- Varchar (variable character): a string of characters with varying length

3. Date and Time Data Types:

- Date: a date value (e.g., YYYY-MM-DD)

- Time: a time value (e.g., HH:MM:SS)

- Timestamp: a date and time value (e.g., YYYY-MM-DD HH:MM:SS)

- Interval: a period of time (e.g., 20 minutes)

4. Boolean Data Type:

- Boolean: true or false values

5. Array Data Type:

- Array: a collection of values of the same data type

6. Composite Data Types:

- Row: a collection of values of different data types

Examples of creating tables with different data types in Java:

```
import java.sql.*;

public class PostgresConnect {
    public static void main(String[] args) {
        final String url = "jdbc:postgresql://localhost/testdb";
        final String user = "postgres";
        final String password = "password";

        try (Connection conn = DriverManager.getConnection(url, user, password);
            Statement statement = conn.createStatement()) {

            String createTableQuery = "CREATE TABLE demo_table " +
                "(id SERIAL PRIMARY KEY, " +
```

```
        "name␣VARCHAR(255),␣" +
        "age␣INT,␣" +
        "dob␣DATE)";

    statement.executeUpdate(createTableQuery);
  } catch (SQLException e) {
    System.out.println("Connection␣failure.");
    e.printStackTrace();
  }
 }
}
```

This example creates a table called "demo_table" with four columns: "id" of type serial (an auto-incrementing integer), "name" of type varchar with a length of 255 characters, "age" of type integer, and "dob" of type date.

2.7 How do you create a new database and user in PostgreSQL?

To create a new database and user in PostgreSQL, you need to follow these steps:

1. Connect to the PostgreSQL server: You can connect to the PostgreSQL server using a command-line tool like 'psql' or a GUI client like pgAdmin.

2. Create a new database: To create a new database, use the 'CREATE DATABASE' command with the desired name of the database. For example, to create a database named "mydb", you can use the following command:

```
CREATE DATABASE mydb;
```

3. Create a new user: To create a new user, use the 'CREATE ROLE' command with the desired username and password. For example, to create a user named "myuser" with password "mypassword", you can use the following command:

```
CREATE ROLE myuser WITH LOGIN PASSWORD 'mypassword';
```

4. Grant permissions: After creating the user, you need to grant appropriate permissions to the user on the newly created database. To

do so, use the 'GRANT' command with the desired permissions. For example, to grant all privileges to the user "myuser" on the database "mydb", you can use the following command:

```
GRANT ALL PRIVILEGES ON DATABASE mydb TO myuser;
```

Once you have created the new database and user, you can connect to the database using the username and password you created, and start using it. Here's an example Java code snippet that demonstrates how to connect to a PostgreSQL database with a specified username and password:

```
import java.sql.*;

public class PostgreSQLExample {
    public static void main(String[] args) {
        Connection conn = null;
        try {
            String url = "jdbc:postgresql://localhost/mydb";
            String username = "myuser";
            String password = "mypassword";
            conn = DriverManager.getConnection(url, username, password);
            System.out.println("Connected_to_the_PostgreSQL_server_successfully
                .");
        } catch (SQLException e) {
            System.out.println(e.getMessage());
        } finally {
            try {
                if (conn != null) {
                    conn.close();
                }
            } catch (SQLException ex) {
                System.out.println(ex.getMessage());
            }
        }
    }
}
```

This code connects to a database named "mydb" on the localhost server using the username and password you created earlier, and prints a success message if the connection is successful.

2.8   How do you connect to a PostgreSQL database using a command-line interface (CLI)?

To connect to a PostgreSQL database using a command-line interface (CLI), you can use the 'psql' command, which is the PostgreSQL interactive terminal. 'psql' is an interactive shell that allows you to interact with the PostgreSQL server and execute SQL commands.

To connect to a PostgreSQL database using 'psql', follow these steps:

1. Open a terminal or command prompt. 2. Type 'psql' followed by the 'user' and 'database' options. You can also specify the 'host' and 'port' options if necessary. For example:

```
psql -U myuser -d mydatabase -h myhost -p 5432
```

Here, 'myuser' is the PostgreSQL username, 'mydatabase' is the name of the database you want to connect to, 'myhost' is the hostname or IP address of the database server, and '5432' is the default PostgreSQL port number.

3. If you are connecting to a remote PostgreSQL server, you may be prompted for a password. Enter the password when prompted.

4. Once you have successfully connected to the database, you can execute SQL commands or interact with the database through the 'psql' command-line interface.

Here's an example Java code that demonstrates how to connect to a PostgreSQL database using the JDBC driver:

```java
import java.sql.*;

public class PostgreSQLJDBC {
    public static void main(String[] args) {
        Connection conn = null;
        try {
            // Register Driver
            Class.forName("org.postgresql.Driver");

            // Open a connection
            conn = DriverManager.getConnection("jdbc:postgresql://localhost:5432/
                mydatabase", "myuser","mypassword");

            // Execute SQL commands
            Statement stmt = conn.createStatement();
            ResultSet rs = stmt.executeQuery("SELECT * FROM mytable");
            while (rs.next()) {
                System.out.println(rs.getString("firstname") + " " + rs.getString("
                    lastname"));
            }
            rs.close();
            stmt.close();
        } catch (Exception e) {
            e.printStackTrace();
        } finally {
            // Close the connection
            try {
```

```
            if (conn != null) {
                conn.close();
            }
        } catch (SQLException e) {
            e.printStackTrace();
        }
    }
  }
}
```

In this example, we first register the JDBC driver for PostgreSQL using the 'Class.forName()' method. Then, we connect to the database
using the 'DriverManager.getConnection()' method and specifying
the JDBC URL, username, and password. After that, we execute
an SQL query using the 'Statement.executeQuery()' method and retrieve the results using a 'ResultSet'. Finally, we close the connection
and handle any exceptions that may occur.

2.9   What is the purpose of an index in PostgreSQL and when should you use it?

In PostgreSQL, an index is a data structure that enables the database
to search and retrieve data from tables in a more efficient way. It does
this by creating a separate data structure that contains pointers to
the actual locations of data in the table, allowing queries to quickly
locate and retrieve data without having to scan through the entire
table.

Indexes are particularly useful for speeding up queries that involve
large amounts of data or complex conditions. For example, if you
have a table with millions of rows and you want to find all the rows
that match a certain condition, using an index can make the search
much faster than scanning through the entire table.

It's important to note that while indexes can improve performance,
they also have some downsides. For one, indexes take up storage
space in the database, and creating too many indexes can impact
performance. Additionally, updating or inserting data into tables
that have indexes can be slower, as the database needs to update the
index as well as the underlying table.

To decide when to use an index, you need to consider the specific characteristics of your database and the types of queries you'll be running. In general, you should use an index when:

1. You're querying a large amount of data, and sorting through it without an index would be too slow

2. You're performing frequent lookups or joins on a particular column or set of columns

3. Your query involves complex conditions that would benefit from an index.

Here's an example of creating an index on a column in PostgreSQL using Java:

```
// Assuming you have already established a connection to a PostgreSQL database

// Create a new index on the "first_name" column of the "users" table
Statement stmt = connection.createStatement();
String sql = "CREATE INDEX idx_users_first_name ON users (first_name)";
stmt.executeUpdate(sql);
```

This would create a new index called "idx_users_first_name" on the "first_name" column of the "users" table, which can then be used to speed up queries that search or sort by first name.

2.10 What is a transaction and how does PostgreSQL handle transactions?

A transaction is a logical unit of work that contains one or more database operations, such as insert, update, or delete. Transactions ensure that all database operations either complete successfully, or the entire set of operations is rolled back to its original state before the entire transaction started.

PostgreSQL supports the standard transaction properties of Atomicity, Consistency, Isolation, and Durability (ACID). This means that a transaction is a single, indivisible unit of work that is either fully executed or not at all. PostgreSQL ensures that transactions are isolated from each other, and that no transaction interferes with others, even when they access the same data concurrently.

To use transactions in PostgreSQL, you need to put your code in a transaction block. For example, in Java, the following code creates a transaction block that inserts two rows into the "my_table" table:

```
try (Connection conn = dataSource.getConnection()) {
    conn.setAutoCommit(false); // start transaction

    try (Statement stmt = conn.createStatement()) {
        stmt.execute("INSERT INTO my_table (col1, col2) VALUES ('value1', 1)");
        stmt.execute("INSERT INTO my_table (col1, col2) VALUES ('value2', 2)");
    }

    conn.commit(); // commit transaction
} catch (SQLException e) {
    conn.rollback(); // rollback transaction
}
```

In this example, we start a transaction block by setting "auto-commit" to false. Then we execute two SQL statements that insert two rows into the "my_table" table. Finally, if there are no exceptions, we commit the transaction, or we rollback the transaction if there is an exception.

PostgreSQL also supports savepoints, which allow you to create nested transactions within a transaction. This feature is useful when you need to roll back only part of a transaction, while leaving the rest intact.

To summarize, PostgreSQL provides full support for transactions and ensures that they are isolated from each other. To use transactions in PostgreSQL, you need to put your code in a transaction block and either commit or rollback the transaction at the end, depending on the success or failure of your database operations.

2.11   Can you explain the difference between DDL, DML, and DCL in PostgreSQL?

In PostgreSQL, like in many other relational database management systems, there are three categories of SQL statements that perform different operations: Data Definition Language (DDL), Data Manipulation Language (DML), and Data Control Language (DCL). Here is a brief explanation of each category:

1. Data Definition Language (DDL): DDL statements are used to define the structure of the database schema, including tables, columns, indexes, and constraints. Examples of DDL statements in PostgreSQL are CREATE, ALTER, and DROP. These statements are used to create and modify database objects.

Example DDL statement:

```
CREATE TABLE users (
  id SERIAL PRIMARY KEY,
  name VARCHAR(50) NOT NULL,
  email VARCHAR(255) UNIQUE NOT NULL
);
```

2. Data Manipulation Language (DML): DML statements are used to manipulate the data stored in the database. Examples of DML statements in PostgreSQL are SELECT, INSERT, UPDATE, and DELETE. These statements are used to add, modify, and remove data from database tables.

Example DML statement:

```
INSERT INTO users (name, email)
VALUES ('John', 'john@example.com');
```

3. Data Control Language (DCL): DCL statements are used to manage the access granted to database users and roles. Examples of DCL statements in PostgreSQL are GRANT and REVOKE. These statements are used to grant and revoke privileges to database objects.

Example DCL statement:

```
GRANT SELECT ON users TO marketing;
```

In summary, DDL is used to define and modify the structure of the database schema, DML is used to manipulate the data stored in the database, and DCL is used to manage the access granted to database users and roles.

2.12   What are the different types of joins in PostgreSQL, and how do they work?

In PostgreSQL, there are several types of joins that can be used to combine data from multiple tables, including:

1. Inner Join

An inner join returns only the rows that have matching values in both tables being joined. It works by comparing the values in the specified columns of each table and returning the rows where those values match. The syntax for an inner join is as follows:

```
SELECT *
FROM table1
JOIN table2
ON table1.column_name = table2.column_name;
```

For example, let's say we have two tables - "employees" and "departments" - and we want to join them based on the "department_id" column:

```
SELECT *
FROM employees
JOIN departments
ON employees.department_id = departments.department_id;
```

This would return only the rows where the "department_id" values match in both tables.

2. Outer Join

An outer join returns all the rows from one table and any matching rows from the other table. There are two types of outer joins:

- Left outer join: returns all the rows from the left table and any matching rows from the right table.

- Right outer join: returns all the rows from the right table and any matching rows from the left table.

The syntax for a left outer join is as follows:

```
SELECT *
FROM table1
LEFT OUTER JOIN table2
ON table1.column_name = table2.column_name;
```

And for a right outer join:

```
SELECT *
FROM table1
RIGHT OUTER JOIN table2
ON table1.column_name = table2.column_name;
```

For example, let's say we have two tables - "orders" and "customers" - and we want to join them based on the "customer_id" column using a left outer join:

```
SELECT *
FROM orders
LEFT OUTER JOIN customers
ON orders.customer_id = customers.customer_id;
```

This would return all the rows from the "orders" table, and any matching rows from the "customers" table. If there are any rows in the "orders" table that don't have a matching row in the "customers" table, those rows will still be included in the result set with NULL values for the "customer" columns.

3. Cross Join

A cross join returns the Cartesian product of the two tables being joined, meaning it returns all possible combinations of rows from both tables. The syntax for a cross join is as follows:

```
SELECT *
FROM table1
CROSS JOIN table2;
```

For example, let's say we have two tables - "colors" and "sizes" - and we want to join them using a cross join:

```
SELECT *
FROM colors
CROSS JOIN sizes;
```

This would return a result set with all possible combinations of rows from the "colors" and "sizes" tables.

4. Self Join

A self join is used when a table needs to be joined with itself. It's useful when a table has a hierarchical relationship and we need to retrieve data from different levels of the hierarchy. The syntax for a

self join is the same as for any other join, but we need to use aliases
to differentiate between the two instances of the same table:

```
SELECT *
FROM table1 AS t1
JOIN table1 AS t2
ON t1.column_name = t2.column_name;
```

For example, let's say we have a table of employees with a "super-
visor_id" column that references the "employee_id" of another employee from the same table. We could use a self join to retrieve the
names of both the employee and their supervisor:

```
SELECT e.employee_name, s.employee_name AS supervisor_name
FROM employees AS e
JOIN employees AS s
ON e.supervisor_id = s.employee_id;
```

This would return a result set with the names of each employee and
their corresponding supervisor.

2.13   What are the aggregate functions available in PostgreSQL, and what are their purposes?

PostgreSQL provides a wide range of aggregate functions to perform
calculations on groups of values rather than individual values returned
by a SELECT statement. The available aggregate functions in PostgreSQL include:

1. AVG(): This function returns the average of a set of values.

Example usage:

```
SELECT AVG(price) FROM products;
```

2. SUM(): This function returns the sum of a set of values.

Example usage:

```
SELECT SUM(quantity) FROM orders;
```

3. MIN(): This function returns the minimum value of a set of values.

Example usage:

```
SELECT MIN(price) FROM products;
```

4. MAX(): This function returns the maximum value of a set of values.

Example usage:

```
SELECT MAX(price) FROM products;
```

5. COUNT(): This function returns the number of rows or non-null values in the specified column.

Example usage:

```
SELECT COUNT(*) FROM users;
```

6. BIT_AND(): This function returns the bitwise AND of all input values.

Example usage:

```
SELECT BIT_AND(value) FROM my_table;
```

7. BIT_OR(): This function returns the bitwise OR of all input values.

Example usage:

```
SELECT BIT_OR(value) FROM my_table;
```

8. BOOL_AND(): This function returns true if all input values are true, and false otherwise.

Example usage:

```
SELECT BOOL_AND(is_active) FROM users;
```

9. BOOL_OR(): This function returns true if at least one input value is true, and false otherwise.

Example usage:

```
SELECT BOOL_OR(is_active) FROM users;
```

10. ARRAY_AGG(): This function returns an array of values for a given column.

Example usage:

```
SELECT ARRAY_AGG(price) FROM products;
```

These are just a few of the aggregate functions provided by PostgreSQL. Each function performs a specific calculation on a set of values, making it easier to retrieve the desired information from your database.

2.14   How do you implement pagination in PostgreSQL to display a limited number of rows per page?

In PostgreSQL, pagination can be implemented using the LIMIT and OFFSET clause in the SELECT query. The LIMIT clause allows you to specify the number of rows to be fetched and the OFFSET clause specifies the number of rows to be skipped.

Let's say we have a table named 'users' with columns 'id', 'name', 'email', and 'age', and we want to display 10 rows per page. The SQL query for the first page would look like this:

```
SELECT id, name, email, age FROM users LIMIT 10 OFFSET 0;
```

This query will fetch the first 10 rows from the 'users' table starting from the first row.

For the second page, we need to skip the first 10 rows and fetch the next 10 rows. The SQL query for the second page would look like this:

```
SELECT id, name, email, age FROM users LIMIT 10 OFFSET 10;
```

This query will fetch the next 10 rows from the 'users' table starting from the 11th row.

To implement pagination in Java, you can use a library like Spring

Data JPA or plain JDBC. Here's an example using plain JDBC:

```java
import java.sql.*;

public class PaginationExample {
    private static final String QUERY = "SELECT id, name, email, age FROM
        users LIMIT ? OFFSET ?;";
    private static final int PAGE_SIZE = 10;

    public static void main(String[] args) throws SQLException {
        int pageNumber = 2;
        int offset = (pageNumber - 1) * PAGE_SIZE;

        try (Connection conn = DriverManager.getConnection("jdbc:postgresql://
            localhost/mydatabase", "myuser", "mypassword");
            PreparedStatement stmt = conn.prepareStatement(QUERY)) {

            stmt.setInt(1, PAGE_SIZE);
            stmt.setInt(2, offset);

            try (ResultSet rs = stmt.executeQuery()) {
                while (rs.next()) {
                    int id = rs.getInt("id");
                    String name = rs.getString("name");
                    String email = rs.getString("email");
                    int age = rs.getInt("age");

                    System.out.printf("%dt%st%st%dn", id, name, email, age);
                }
            }
        }
    }
}
```

In this example, we calculate the offset based on the page number and multiply it by the page size. Then we set the parameters for the prepared statement using the 'setInt' method, and execute the query using the 'executeQuery' method. Finally, we loop through the ResultSet and retrieve the values for each column using the 'getInt' and 'getString' methods.

2.15 What is the difference between a view and a table in PostgreSQL, and when should you use each one?

In PostgreSQL, a table is a collection of data stored in a structured format with columns and rows, while a view is a virtual table created based on the result set of a predefined SQL query.

When you have a large amount of data that needs to be stored and accessed frequently, a table is the best option. You can create new tables, modify their contents, add or remove rows, and perform complex queries on them easily. Here is an example of creating a table in PostgreSQL using Java:

```
try (Connection conn = DriverManager.getConnection(url, username, password);
     Statement stmt = conn.createStatement()) {
    String createTable = "CREATE TABLE myTable (id SERIAL PRIMARY KEY, name
        VARCHAR(50), age INT)";
    stmt.executeUpdate(createTable);
}
```

On the other hand, a view is a virtual table that is derived from one or more tables or other views. Views do not store data separately; rather, they provide a mechanism to retrieve data from existing tables and customize it according to specific requirements. Views have the advantage of simplifying access to frequently used data, hiding the complexity of underlying tables, and providing an additional level of security by restricting the views access to the underlying tables. Here is an example of creating a view in PostgreSQL using Java:

```
try (Connection conn = DriverManager.getConnection(url, username, password);
     Statement stmt = conn.createStatement()) {
    String createView = "CREATE VIEW myView AS SELECT name, age FROM myTable
        WHERE age > 20";
    stmt.executeUpdate(createView);
}
```

In summary, use a table when you need to store a large amount of data that requires frequent processing and modification, and use a view when you need to simplify access to data by creating a virtual table that hides the complexity of underlying tables or restricts access to sensitive data.

2.16   How do you perform a basic SELECT query in PostgreSQL, including filtering, sorting, and limiting results?

Performing a basic SELECT query in PostgreSQL is easy. Here is an example of a SELECT statement that retrieves all rows from a table named "employees":

```
SELECT * FROM employees;
```

To filter the results of the SELECT statement based on a condition, you can use the WHERE clause. Here is an example of how to retrieve employees where the salary is greater or equal to $50,000:

```
SELECT * FROM employees WHERE salary >= 50000;
```

To sort the results of the SELECT statement, you can use the ORDER BY clause. Here is an example of how to sort employees by their last name:

```
SELECT * FROM employees ORDER BY last_name;
```

You can specify the sort order, either ascending or descending, by using the ASC or DESC keyword, respectively. Here is an example of how to sort employees by salary in descending order:

```
SELECT * FROM employees ORDER BY salary DESC;
```

To limit the number of results returned by the SELECT statement, you can use the LIMIT clause. Here is an example of how to retrieve the first 10 employees from the table:

```
SELECT * FROM employees LIMIT 10;
```

You can also use the OFFSET clause to skip a certain number of rows before starting to return results. Here is an example of how to retrieve the next 10 employees after skipping the first 10:

```
SELECT * FROM employees OFFSET 10 LIMIT 10;
```

These clauses can be combined in various ways to make complex queries that retrieve only the data you need.

2.17   What is the purpose of the WHERE clause in PostgreSQL, and how does it work?

The WHERE clause in PostgreSQL is used to filter rows from a table based on specified conditions. It follows the SELECT statement and is followed by any other clauses like ORDER BY or GROUP BY clauses.

The basic syntax of the WHERE clause is as follows:

```
SELECT column1, column2, ...
FROM table_name
WHERE condition;
```

The condition is the expression that evaluates to true or false for each row in the table. Rows that evaluate to true are included in the query results, while rows that evaluate to false are excluded.

Here's an example that demonstrates how the WHERE clause works in PostgreSQL:

Suppose we have a table called employees, which contains information about employees in a company. We want to retrieve a list of all employees whose age is greater than or equal to 30. The query would be as follows:

```
SELECT *
FROM employees
WHERE age >= 30;
```

In this example, the 'age >= 30' condition is evaluated for each row in the employees table. Only rows that satisfy the condition are included in the query result.

So, the WHERE clause can be used to filter rows based on various conditions such as greater than or equal to, less than or equal to, not equal to, or any other logical operators. It can also be combined with AND, OR and NOT operators to form complex conditions.

2.18   Can you explain the difference between GROUP BY and ORDER BY in PostgreSQL?

GROUP BY and ORDER BY are both clauses that are commonly used in SELECT statements in PostgreSQL, but they serve different purposes.

GROUP BY is used to group rows that have the same values in a specified column or columns. When a GROUP BY clause is included in a statement, the result set is divided into groups, and each group represents a unique set of values in the selected columns. An aggregate function, such as SUM or COUNT, is usually used with GROUP BY to perform calculations on each group.

For example, suppose we have a table named sales that contains information about sales made by a company, including the date, the product name, and the amount sold. We might want to group the sales data by product name and calculate the total amount of each product sold. Here's how we could use GROUP BY to do that:

```
SELECT product_name, SUM(amount_sold)
FROM sales
GROUP BY product_name;
```

This statement will return a result set that shows the product name and the total amount sold for each product.

ORDER BY, on the other hand, is used to sort the result set on one or more columns. By default, ORDER BY sorts the results in ascending order, but you can also specify DESC to sort in descending order.

For example, suppose we want to order the sales data by the amount sold, from highest to lowest. Here's how we could use ORDER BY:

```
SELECT product_name, SUM(amount_sold)
FROM sales
GROUP BY product_name
ORDER BY SUM(amount_sold) DESC;
```

This statement will return the same result set as before, but the results will be sorted by the total amount sold in descending order.

To summarize:

- GROUP BY is used to group the rows in the result set based on values in one or more columns, and is usually used with aggregate functions.

- ORDER BY is used to sort the rows in the result set on one or more columns.

I hope this helps clarify the difference between GROUP BY and ORDER BY in PostgreSQL!

2.19   How do you create and use stored procedures and functions in PostgreSQL?

Stored procedures and functions are database objects that are used to encapsulate and execute a series of database operations. In Post-greSQL, stored procedures and functions can be created and used to simplify complex operations or business logic that require multiple SQL statements executed sequentially.

To create a stored procedure or function in PostgreSQL, you need to follow these steps:

1. Connect to your PostgreSQL database using a PostgreSQL client such as psql or pgAdmin.

2. Create a function using the CREATE FUNCTION statement. This statement includes the name of the function, list of parameters, and the function body. Below is an example:

```
CREATE FUNCTION get_employee_salary(emp_id INT) RETURNS NUMERIC AS $$
DECLARE
    salary NUMERIC;
BEGIN
    SELECT salary INTO salary FROM employees WHERE id = emp_id;
    RETURN salary;
END;
$$ LANGUAGE plpgsql;
```

In this example, the function 'get_employee_salary' takes an input parameter 'emp_id' of type 'INT' and returns 'NUMERIC' data type. The function retrieves the salary of an employee with the given 'id' from the 'employees' table and returns it.

3. Once the function is created, you can call it using the SELECT statement. Below is an example:

```
SELECT get_employee_salary(1001);
```

This will return the salary of the employee with 'id' 1001.

Now let's look at how to create a stored procedure:

1. Connect to your PostgreSQL database using a PostgreSQL client such as psql or pgAdmin.

2. Create a stored procedure using the CREATE PROCEDURE state-

ment. This statement includes the name of the procedure, list of parameters, and the procedure body. Below is an example:

```
CREATE PROCEDURE update_employee_salary(emp_id INT, new_salary NUMERIC)
LANGUAGE plpgsql
AS $$
BEGIN
    UPDATE employees SET salary = new_salary WHERE id = emp_id;
END;
$$;
```

In this example, the stored procedure 'update_employee_salary' takes two input parameters 'emp_id' and 'new_salary', both of which are of type 'INT' and 'NUMERIC' respectively. The procedure updates the salary of an employee with the given 'id' to the new salary value.

3. Once the procedure is created, you can call it using the CALL statement. Below is an example:

```
CALL update_employee_salary(1001, 75000.00);
```

This will update the salary of the employee with 'id' 1001 to 75000.00.

In summary, stored procedures and functions in PostgreSQL make it possible to encapsulate complex database operations or business logic. They can be created and used easily using PostgreSQL client tools such as psql or pgAdmin, and the PL/pgSQL language provides a powerful and flexible way to define them.

2.20 What are triggers in PostgreSQL, and what are some common use cases for them?

In PostgreSQL, a trigger is a set of instructions that can be automatically executed by the database when certain events occur on a table, view or schema. The events supported by PostgreSQL triggers are:

- BEFORE INSERT

- AFTER INSERT

- BEFORE UPDATE

- AFTER UPDATE

- BEFORE DELETE

- AFTER DELETE

When any of these events occur on a table, view or schema, the corresponding trigger is executed, allowing the execution of additional operations alongside the original query.

For example, let's say that we have a table 'employees' that includes columns for 'name', 'salary', and 'hire_date'. We can define a trigger on the 'employees' table that will automatically update the 'hire_date' column whenever a new employee is inserted. Here's an example:

```
CREATE TRIGGER update_hire_date
BEFORE INSERT ON employees
FOR EACH ROW
EXECUTE FUNCTION update_hire_date_function();
```

In this example, we've defined a trigger named 'update_hire_date' that will execute a function called 'update_hire_date_function()' before every 'INSERT' operation on the 'employees' table. Inside the function, we can update the 'hire_date' column to the current date and time, like this:

```
CREATE FUNCTION update_hire_date_function()
RETURNS TRIGGER AS $$
BEGIN
  NEW.hire_date := NOW();
  RETURN NEW;
END;
$$ LANGUAGE plpgsql;
```

This example trigger will ensure that the 'hire_date' column is automatically updated whenever a new employee is added to the 'employees' table.

Some common use cases for PostgreSQL triggers include:

- Enforcing data integrity: Triggers can be used to validate data before it is inserted, updated or deleted from a table, ensuring that data remains consistent and correct.

- Auditing changes: Triggers can be used to track changes to tables, views or schemas, allowing administrators to monitor the history of changes and identify potential security risks.

- Synchronizing data: Triggers can be used to update data across multiple tables or databases, ensuring that data remains consistent across the enterprise.

- Implementing business rules: Triggers can be used to enforce business rules and processes, for example, by automatically sending notifications or alerts when data meets certain criteria.

Overall, triggers are a powerful and flexible tool that can be used to implement a wide range of functionality in PostgreSQL databases.

Chapter 3

Intermediate

3.1 What is the ACID property in databases, and how does PostgreSQL ensure ACID compliance?

ACID stands for Atomicity, Consistency, Isolation, and Durability. These are the four key properties that a database system must exhibit to ensure transactional reliability and consistency.

Atomicity means that a transaction is treated as a single, all-or-nothing operation, ensuring that the transaction either completely succeeds or completely fails.

Consistency ensures that after a transaction, the database is in a consistent state, meaning that all data integrity constraints are satisfied.

Isolation implies that concurrent transactions do not interfere with each other. This ensures that multiple transactions may occur simultaneously without interfering with each other.

Durability ensures that once a transaction is committed, its effects are permanent in the face of any subsequent failure.

PostgreSQL ensures ACID compliance with its transaction processing system. PostgreSQL ensures atomicity by providing the ROLLBACK command, which can undo all changes made by a transaction.

Consistency is ensured through the use of constraints, such as foreign keys, unique constraints, and check constraints. PostgreSQL includes support for declarative referential integrity (DRI) which is designed to enforce the consistency of the data.

Isolation is achieved through the use of locks, which ensure that concurrent transactions do not interfere with each other. PostgreSQL provides several isolation levels, which allow you to tune the trade-offs between the desire for consistency in the face of concurrency and performance.

Durability is ensured by writing data to disk, ensuring that the data can be recovered in the event of a system crash or other catastrophic failure.

Here's an example Java code that demonstrates how PostgreSQL's transaction processing system ensures atomicity and consistency:

```
Connection connection = DriverManager.getConnection("jdbc:postgresql://
    localhost/mydatabase", "username", "password");
connection.setAutoCommit(false); // start transaction

try {
    PreparedStatement statement1 = connection.prepareStatement("INSERT INTO
        employees (name, salary) VALUES (?, ?)");
    statement1.setString(1, "John Doe");
    statement1.setDouble(2, 50000.00);
    statement1.executeUpdate();

    PreparedStatement statement2 = connection.prepareStatement("INSERT INTO
        benefits (employee_id, health_insurance) VALUES (?, ?)");
    statement2.setInt(1, 1); // assuming the employee_id is 1
    statement2.setBoolean(2, true);
    statement2.executeUpdate();

    connection.commit(); // commit the transaction
} catch (SQLException ex) {
    connection.rollback(); // rollback the transaction in case an exception
        occurs
} finally {
    connection.setAutoCommit(true); // set autocommit to true
}
```

In this example, a transaction is started by setting 'setAutoCommit' to 'false'. Two 'INSERT' statements are executed to insert data into two tables. If any exception occurs, the transaction is rolled back using 'rollback()'. Otherwise, the transaction is committed using 'commit()'. This ensures that the data is either inserted into both tables or neither table, ensuring atomicity. In addition, the consistency of the data is ensured through constraints and foreign keys defined in the schema.

3.2 Explain the concept of MVCC (Multi-Version Concurrency Control) in PostgreSQL and how it affects transaction isolation.

MVCC (Multi-Version Concurrency Control) is a mechanism used by PostgreSQL to provide concurrent access to the database while ensuring transaction isolation. It allows multiple transactions to read and write data without blocking each other.

Under MVCC, each transaction sees a snapshot of the database at a specific point in time. Whenever a transaction modifies a row in a table, PostgreSQL creates a new copy of the row instead of overwriting the existing row. This new copy is assigned a unique transaction ID, which is used to track changes made to the row.

When a transaction reads a row, it sees the copy that was valid at the time the transaction started, based on its transaction ID. This ensures that the transaction sees a consistent view of the database, without being affected by changes made by other transactions that are still in progress.

To understand how MVCC affects transaction isolation, consider the following scenario:

- Transaction A begins and reads a row with ID 1

- Transaction B begins and updates the row with ID 1

- Transaction A continues and updates the row with ID 1

Under MVCC, transaction A and B each see a snapshot of the database at a specific point in time. When transaction B updates the row with ID 1, it creates a new copy of the row with a unique transaction ID. Transaction A, however, still sees the original version of the row with its own unique transaction ID. When transaction A updates the row, it creates yet another copy with a unique transaction ID.

This means that when the transactions commit, PostgreSQL must reconcile the changes made to the row by each transaction. If the changes do not conflict, they can be merged together. If they conflict, one of the transactions must be rolled back.

MVCC in PostgreSQL helps to ensure that transactions do not block each other unnecessarily, improving performance and scalability. It also provides a high degree of transaction isolation, allowing transactions to operate in a consistent state without being affected by the changes made by other transactions.

3.3   What is the difference between the VACUUM and ANALYZE operations in PostgreSQL, and when should you use them?

VACUUM and ANALYZE are two separate operations in PostgreSQL, although they are often performed together.

VACUUM is a maintenance operation in PostgreSQL that reclaims storage space and defragments tables by removing dead rows and optimizing table layouts. Dead rows are rows that are no longer visible or used in any transactions because they have been updated or deleted but still exist in the table. Vacuuming can help reduce table bloat, which can slow down query performance and increase disk usage.

There are several types of VACUUM operations that can be performed:

- FULL VACUUM: Reclaims all expired rows and shrinks the table to its minimum size. This operation requires an exclusive lock on the table and can take a long time to complete, especially on large tables.
- FREEZE: Marks all tuples older than the current transaction ID as frozen, preventing them from being vacuumed until all transaction IDs are older than the frozen ones. This operation can help reduce the need for regular vacuuming and improve read performance.
- ANALYZE: Updates the database statistics for the table, which is used by the query planner to determine the most efficient execution plan for a given query.

ANALYZE is the operation that updates the database statistics for a given table to help the query planner generate more efficient execution plans. The statistics include details like the number of rows, the distribution of values in the columns, and whether an index is used or not. Without up-to-date statistics, the query planner may choose inefficient query plans, resulting in slow performance.

In general, you should use VACUUM regularly to help maintain the health and performance of your PostgreSQL database. By default, PostgreSQL runs vacuuming automatically in the background, but you may need to manually run vacuum when there is significant table bloat or after a large number of updates or deletes. You should also use ANALYZE periodically, especially after significant changes to the schema or data, to ensure the query planner has accurate statistics to generate optimal query plans.

Here's an example of how to manually run VACUUM and ANALYZE on a table in Java using JDBC:

```
Connection conn = DriverManager.getConnection("jdbc:postgresql://localhost/
    mydb", "myuser", "mypassword");
String table = "mytable";

// Run VACUUM
Statement vacuumStmt = conn.createStatement();
vacuumStmt.execute("VACUUM " + table);

// Run ANALYZE
Statement analyzeStmt = conn.createStatement();
analyzeStmt.execute("ANALYZE " + table);
```

Note that this is just a basic example, and you should always be careful when running vacuuming operations on large tables, as they can take a significant amount of time and block other transactions.

3.4 How do you perform a backup and restore of a PostgreSQL database using pg_dump and pg_restore?

Performing a backup and restore of a PostgreSQL database can be a straightforward process when using the 'pg_dump' and 'pg_restore' utilities. The following steps detail the process:

1. **Perform a backup with pg_dump:** The 'pg_dump' utility is used to create a backup of the PostgreSQL database. A database can be backed up in several formats, including plain SQL, custom or directory format. The recommended option is the custom format which provides better compression and can be faster to restore. The following code snippet shows how to perform a backup with 'pg_dump':

```
public static void performBackup() throws IOException {
    ProcessBuilder pb = new ProcessBuilder("/usr/bin/pg_dump", "-Fc", "-f", "/
        path/to/backup_file.backup", "database_name");
    pb.environment().put("PGPASSWORD", "database_password");
    pb.start();
    System.out.println("Backup completed successfully.");
}
```

In this example, the command 'pg_dump -Fc -f /path/to/backup_file.backup database_name' is executed using 'ProcessBuilder'. The '-Fc' option indicates that the backup will be in custom format, '-f /path/to/backup_file.backup' specifies the path and file name for the backup, and 'database_name' is the name of the database to be backed up. The 'PGPASSWORD' environment variable is set to provide the password for the database.

2. **Perform a restore with pg_restore:** The 'pg_restore' utility is used to restore a database from a backup file. The following code snippet shows how to restore a database with 'pg_restore':

```
public static void performRestore() throws IOException {
    ProcessBuilder pb = new ProcessBuilder("/usr/bin/pg_restore", "-c", "-O",
        "-d", "database_name", "/path/to/backup_file.backup");
    pb.environment().put("PGPASSWORD", "database_password");
    pb.start();
    System.out.println("Restore completed successfully.");
}
```

In this example, the command 'pg_restore -c -O -d database_name /path/to/backup_file.backup' is executed using 'ProcessBuilder'. The '-c' option drops the database objects before recreating them, '-O' skips restoring the ownership of the objects, and '-d database_name' specifies the destination database for restoring. The 'PGPASSWORD' environment variable is set to provide the password for the database.

These are basic examples to illustrate the process; you may need to adjust the details depending on your specific environment and requirements. It is also worth noting that the 'pg_dump' and 'pg_restore' utilities can be used with various options and flags that can provide greater flexibility and control over the backup and restore process.

Full details can be found in the PostgreSQL documentation.

3.5 Explain the role of the Write-Ahead Log (WAL) in PostgreSQL and how it contributes to data durability.

In PostgreSQL, the Write-Ahead Log (WAL) is a mechanism used to ensure data durability by logging all changes to the database before they are applied. The purpose of WAL is to provide a reliable mechanism for recovering data in case of a crash or other system failure.

When data is written to PostgreSQL, it is first written to a buffer in memory. The WAL then records the changes that have been made to the buffer using a sequential log of transactions. As new transactions are written to the log, the system periodically flushes changes in the buffer to disk. In the event of a system failure, the database can use the WAL to recover lost data by replaying the log and restoring the database to a consistent state.

The WAL also provides other benefits beyond data durability. For example, it can be used to replicate data to other servers, allowing for high-availability and fault tolerance. It can also be used to optimize performance by reducing the number of synchronization points needed when writing to disk.

Here is an example Java code that shows how to perform a simple update on a table and how WAL logs are generated:

```
Connection conn = DriverManager.getConnection(url, user, password);
Statement stmt = conn.createStatement();
String sql = "UPDATE users SET name = 'Alice' WHERE id = 1;";
stmt.executeUpdate(sql);
```

In this example, we connect to our PostgreSQL database using the JDBC driver. We then create a new SQL statement to update the 'users' table, setting the 'name' field to 'Alice' for the row with an 'id' of '1'.

After the statement is executed, PostgreSQL records the changes in the WAL by appending the transaction to the WAL log files. This ensures that the changes are written to disk before committing the transaction. If the system crashes before the changes are fully written to disk, the WAL can be replayed to recover the data.

3.6   How do you create and manage database indexes in PostgreSQL to optimize query performance?

In PostgreSQL, you can create indexes on tables to optimize query performance. These indexes help the database server quickly find the rows that match a query's WHERE clause, GROUP BY clause, or ORDER BY clause. Here are the steps to create and manage indexes in PostgreSQL:

1. Create an index: To create an index, you can use the CREATE INDEX statement. For example, to create an index on a table's "name" column, you can use the following SQL:

```
CREATE INDEX idx_name ON table_name (name);
```

This will create an index named "idx_name" on the "name" column of the "table_name" table. You can also create a unique index to enforce uniqueness on a column or group of columns:

```
CREATE UNIQUE INDEX idx_unique_name ON table_name (name);
```

2. View existing indexes: You can view the existing indexes on a table using the following SQL:

```
SELECT * FROM pg_indexes WHERE tablename = 'table_name';
```

This will show you all the indexes on the "table_name" table. You can also view the indexes on a specific column using the following SQL:

```
SELECT * FROM pg_indexes WHERE tablename = 'table_name' AND indexdef ILIKE '%
    name%';
```

This will show you all the indexes on the "table_name" table that involve the "name" column.

3. Drop an index: If you no longer need an index, you can drop it using the DROP INDEX statement. For example, to drop the "idx_name" index, you can use the following SQL:

```
DROP INDEX idx_name;
```

4. Analyze tables: PostgreSQL uses statistics to determine the most optimal query execution plan. Running an ANALYZE command on a table updates the statistics for that table, which can help PostgreSQL choose a better execution plan. You can use the following SQL to analyze a table:

```
ANALYZE table_name;
```

5. Monitor index usage: You can monitor the usage of your indexes using the pg_stat_user_indexes view. This view provides statistics on the number of times an index has been used, the number of tuples fetched using the index, and the size of the index in memory. For example, to view the usage statistics for the "idx_name" index, you can use the following SQL:

```
SELECT * FROM pg_stat_user_indexes WHERE indexname = 'idx_name';
```

6. Use explain analyze: Finally, you can use the EXPLAIN ANALYZE command to see how PostgreSQL is executing your queries. This command shows you the query execution plan and the time taken to execute each step. By analyzing the output of this command, you can identify queries that are not using your indexes efficiently, and make optimization adjustments accordingly.

Here's some example Java code that demonstrates how to create an index in PostgreSQL using the JDBC driver:

```java
try (Connection conn = DriverManager.getConnection(url, username, password);
    Statement stmt = conn.createStatement()) {

    // Create an index on the "name" column
    stmt.execute("CREATE INDEX idx_name ON table_name (name)");

} catch (SQLException e) {
    // Handle errors
}
```

In summary, creating and managing indexes in PostgreSQL involves creating the index, viewing existing indexes, dropping an index, analyzing tables, monitoring index usage, and using explain analyze to

analyze query execution plans. These techniques can help you optimize query performance for your PostgreSQL database.

3.7 What are the different types of locking mechanisms in PostgreSQL and how do they work?

PostgreSQL provides several types of locking mechanisms that allow
for safe and concurrent access to a database. Let's dive into each type
of lock and how they work in detail.

1. Row-level locking:
As the name suggests, this type of locking mechanism works at the
row level. It grants exclusive access to a particular row in a table and
locks it for other transactions. This lock is only released when the
transaction that placed the lock is committed or rolled back.

For example, let's say that a table 'books' has multiple rows, and two
transactions started executing simultaneously, and the first transaction executed the following SQL statement "'SELECT * FROM books
WHERE id = 1 FOR UPDATE'." This statement will lock the row
with 'id = 1' for the first transaction, and the second transaction
that tries to access this row will be blocked until the first transaction
releases the lock.

Here is how this would look like in Java code:

```
try (Connection conn = DriverManager.getConnection(url, user, password);
     PreparedStatement stmt = conn.prepareStatement("SELECT * FROM books
          WHERE id = ? FOR UPDATE")) {
     stmt.setInt(1, 1);
     ResultSet rs = stmt.executeQuery();
     while (rs.next()) {
         // your code goes here
     }
} catch (SQLException e) {
     // handle SQL exception
}
```

2. Table-level locking:
This type of locking mechanism locks the entire table, and no other
transaction can access the table until the lock is released. This lock
only releases when the transaction that holds the lock is committed

or rolled back.

For example, let's say there are two transactions that try to access a table 'books', and the first transaction executes "'LOCK TABLE books IN SHARE MODE;'" statement. This statement locks the entire table in shared mode, allowing other transactions to read data but not modify it. The second transaction that tries to perform any operation on the 'books' table will be blocked until the first transaction releases the lock.

Here is how this would look like in Java code:

```
try (Connection conn = DriverManager.getConnection(url, user, password);
    PreparedStatement stmt = conn.prepareStatement("LOCK TABLE books IN
        SHARE MODE")) {
        stmt.executeUpdate();
} catch (SQLException e) {
    // handle SQL exception
}
```

3. Predicate Locking:
This type of locking mechanism allows you to lock specific rows based on a specific condition mentioned in the SQL statement. PostgreSQL uses the WHERE clause to determine the rows to be locked, and this lock only lasts until the next row in the database is fetched.

For example, let's say that two transactions are trying to update a table 'books'. Transaction A is executing the SQL statement "'UPDATE books SET price = 800 WHERE author = 'JK Rowling';'" while transaction B executes "'UPDATE books SET price = 900 WHERE author = 'JK Rowling';'" Both the transactions will acquire a predicate lock on all rows with 'author = 'JK Rowling''.

Here is how this would look like in Java code:

```
try (Connection conn = DriverManager.getConnection(url, user, password);
    PreparedStatement stmt = conn.prepareStatement("UPDATE books SET price=
        ? WHERE author = ?")) {
        stmt.setInt(1, 800);
        stmt.setString(2, "JK Rowling");
        stmt.executeUpdate();
} catch (SQLException e) {
    // handle SQL exception
}
```

In conclusion, PostgreSQL provides several types of locking mechanisms to ensure safe and concurrent access to the database, and understanding these locking mechanisms is essential for designing robust and scalable applications.

3.8   Explain the concept of prepared statements in PostgreSQL and their benefits.

Prepared statements in PostgreSQL are pre-compiled SQL statements that can be used multiple times with different parameter values. These statements are compiled by the server and stored in a cache so that they can be reused without the need for recompilation.

The benefits of using prepared statements in PostgreSQL are as follows:

1. Performance: Prepared statements can improve performance because they reduce the overhead of parsing, analyzing, and optimizing SQL statements. This is especially true for complex queries.

2. Security: Prepared statements can help prevent SQL injection attacks by separating the SQL code from the data values. Since the parameters are passed separately from the SQL code, there is no possibility for an attacker to inject malicious code into the statements.

3. Maintainable code: Prepared statements can make code more maintainable because they separate SQL code from application code. This makes it easier to update and modify the SQL code without affecting the application code.

Here is an example of using prepared statements in Java for PostgreSQL:

```
// Connection initialization
Connection connection = DriverManager.getConnection("jdbc:postgresql://
    localhost/testdb", "username", "password");

// Prepare a statement
PreparedStatement preparedStatement = connection.prepareStatement("SELECT *
    FROM users WHERE name = ?");

// Set parameter values
preparedStatement.setString(1, "John");

// Execute the query
ResultSet resultSet = preparedStatement.executeQuery();
```

```
// Process the result set
while (resultSet.next()) {
    System.out.println(resultSet.getString("name"));
}

// Close the resources
resultSet.close();
preparedStatement.close();
connection.close();
```

In this example, we prepare a statement to select users with a specific name. We then set the parameter value to 'John' and execute the query using 'executeQuery()' method. Finally, we process the result set and close the resources. This code can be reused with different parameter values for different queries, and thus can improve performance and reduce security risks.

3.9 What is the difference between UNION, UNION ALL, INTERSECT, and EXCEPT operations in PostgreSQL?

In PostgreSQL, UNION, UNION ALL, INTERSECT, and EXCEPT are set operations used to combine or compare the results of multiple SELECT statements.

1. UNION: The UNION operation combines the results of two or more SELECT statements, removing any duplicate rows. It is similar to combining the results of two tables using the SQL JOIN operation. The syntax for UNION is as follows:

```
SELECT column1, column2, ... FROM table1
UNION
SELECT column1, column2, ... FROM table2
```

Example:

Suppose we have two tables named "students" and "teachers". Both tables have the columns "name" and "age".

```
students
--------
name | age
-----|-----
John | 18
Sara | 19
```

```
Tom  | 20

teachers
--------
name | age
------|-----
Emily | 30
Tom   | 40
```

If we want to combine the names of students and teachers without any duplicates, we can use the UNION operation as follows:

```
SELECT name FROM students
UNION
SELECT name FROM teachers
```

The output of this query would be:

```
name
------
Emily
John
Sara
Tom
```

As we can see, the duplicate name "Tom" has been removed from the result set.

2. UNION ALL: The UNION ALL operation combines the results of two or more SELECT statements, including duplicate rows. The syntax for UNION ALL is the same as for UNION, except we use the keyword UNION ALL instead of UNION. Example:

```
SELECT name FROM students
UNION ALL
SELECT name FROM teachers
```

The output of this query would be:

```
name
------
John
Sara
Tom
Emily
Tom
```

As we can see, the duplicate name "Tom" appears twice in the result set.

3. INTERSECT: The INTERSECT operation returns only the rows that are common to both SELECT statements. In other words, it re-

turns the intersection of two result sets. The syntax for INTERSECT is as follows:

```
SELECT column1, column2, ... FROM table1
INTERSECT
SELECT column1, column2, ... FROM table2
```

Example:

Suppose we have two tables named "table1" and "table2". Both tables have the columns "id" and "name".

```
table1
-------
id | name
---|-----
1  | A
2  | B
3  | C

table2
-------
id | name
---|-----
2  | B
3  | C
4  | D
```

If we want to find the rows that are common to both tables based on the "id" column, we can use the INTERSECT operation as follows:

```
SELECT id, name FROM table1
INTERSECT
SELECT id, name FROM table2
```

The output of this query would be:

```
id | name
---|-----
2  | B
3  | C
```

As we can see, only the rows with "id" 2 and 3 are common to both tables.

4. EXCEPT: The EXCEPT operation returns only the rows that are in the first SELECT statement but not in the second SELECT statement. In other words, it returns the set difference between two result sets. The syntax for EXCEPT is as follows:

```
SELECT column1, column2, ... FROM table1
EXCEPT
SELECT column1, column2, ... FROM table2
```

Example:

Suppose we have the same two tables as in the previous example.

If we want to find the rows that are in "table1" but not in "table2" based on the "id" column, we can use the EXCEPT operation as follows:

```
SELECT id, name FROM table1
EXCEPT
SELECT id, name FROM table2
```

The output of this query would be:

```
id | name
---|-----
1  | A
```

As we can see, only the row with "id" 1 is in "table1" but not in "table2".

3.10   How do you set up and manage replication in PostgreSQL for high availability and load balancing?

Setting up and managing replication in PostgreSQL involves creating and configuring a replica server (or servers) that will receive and replicate changes made on the primary server. This can provide high availability and load balancing capabilities for your database system.

Here are the general steps to set up and manage replication in PostgreSQL:

1. Choose a replication method: PostgreSQL supports several types of replication methods, including physical streaming replication, logical replication, and trigger-based replication. Each method has its own benefits and drawbacks, so it's important to choose the one that best fits your needs.

2. Set up a primary server: This server will be the source of all changes that will be replicated to the replica server(s). You will need

to set up the server, configure the database and tables, and ensure that the necessary permissions are in place.

3. Set up a replica server: The replica server will receive and replicate changes made on the primary server. You will need to set up a new instance of PostgreSQL on the replica server, configure the replication settings, and ensure that the server is capable of handling the replicated data.

4. Configure replication settings: In PostgreSQL, replication settings are configured in the 'postgresql.conf' file and the 'pg_hba.conf' file. You will need to ensure that these settings are configured correctly for both the primary and replica servers.

5. Set up replication slots: A replication slot is a logical mechanism that allows the replica server to request and receive changes from the primary server. You will need to create a replication slot on the primary server and specify the slot's name and replication method.

6. Start replication: Once everything is set up and configured correctly, you can start replication by running the 'pg_basebackup' command on the replica server. This will create an initial copy of the database from the primary server, and then the replica server will begin receiving and replicating changes made on the primary server.

It's important to note that managing replication in PostgreSQL requires ongoing maintenance and monitoring. You should regularly check the replica server for consistency and ensure that it is up to date with the primary server. Additionally, you should have a plan in place for failover and disaster recovery in case the primary server goes down or becomes unavailable.

Here's an example of how to set up physical streaming replication in PostgreSQL using Java:

```
// Set up the primary server
String primaryUrl = "jdbc:postgresql://primary.server.com/dbname";
Properties primaryProps = new Properties();
primaryProps.setProperty("user", "username");
primaryProps.setProperty("password", "password");
Connection primaryConn = DriverManager.getConnection(primaryUrl, primaryProps
    );

// Set up the replica server
String replicaUrl = "jdbc:postgresql://replica.server.com/dbname";
Properties replicaProps = new Properties();
replicaProps.setProperty("user", "username");
```

```
replicaProps.setProperty("password", "password");
ReplicationConnection replicaConn = ReplicationDriver.connect(replicaUrl,
    replicaProps);

// Set up replication settings
String slotName = "replica_slot";
ReplicationStream stream = replicaConn
    .replicationStream()
    .physical()
    .withSlotName(slotName)
    .withNodeName("replica_node")
    .withStartPosition(LogSequenceNumber.WAL_START)
    .start();

// Start replication
while (true) {
    ByteBuffer msg = stream.readPending();
    if (msg == null) {
        try {
            Thread.sleep(10);
        } catch (InterruptedException e) {
            // Handle exception
        }
    } else {
        // Process replicated changes
    }
}
```

This Java code sets up a connection to the primary server and replica
server, configures replication settings, and starts replication using
physical streaming replication. It uses the JDBC driver for PostgreSQL and the 'pgjdbc-ng' library for replication. Note that this is
just an example, and replication settings and configuration may vary
depending on your specific setup and requirements.

3.11   What are the different types of constraints in PostgreSQL, and how do they help maintain data integrity?

PostgreSQL supports several types of constraints for maintaining data
integrity. Constraints are used to define rules or conditions that must
be satisfied before data can be inserted, updated or deleted from a
table. The following are the most common types of constraints in
PostgreSQL:

1. NOT NULL Constraint: The NOT NULL constraint ensures that
a column cannot contain a null value. If a user tries to insert a
NULL value into a column that has a NOT NULL constraint on it,

PostgreSQL will raise an error.

Here is an example of defining a NOT NULL constraint in a table creation statement:

```
CREATE TABLE students (
    id serial PRIMARY KEY,
    name varchar NOT NULL,
    age integer,
    class varchar
);
```

In this example, the "name" column has a NOT NULL constraint defined on it.

2. UNIQUE Constraint: The UNIQUE constraint ensures that each value in a column is unique across all rows in the table. If a user tries to insert a duplicate value into a column that has a UNIQUE constraint on it, PostgreSQL will raise an error.

Here is an example of defining a UNIQUE constraint in a table creation statement:

```
CREATE TABLE students (
    id serial PRIMARY KEY,
    name varchar UNIQUE,
    age integer,
    class varchar
);
```

In this example, the "name" column has a UNIQUE constraint defined on it.

3. PRIMARY KEY Constraint: The PRIMARY KEY constraint is used to uniquely identify each row in a table. It is a combination of the NOT NULL and UNIQUE constraints, as it ensures that each value is unique and cannot be NULL.

Here is an example of defining a PRIMARY KEY constraint in a table creation statement:

```
CREATE TABLE students (
    id serial PRIMARY KEY,
    name varchar,
    age integer,
    class varchar
);
```

In this example, the "id" column has a PRIMARY KEY constraint defined on it.

4. FOREIGN KEY Constraint: The FOREIGN KEY constraint is used to establish a link between two tables. It ensures that the values in a column of one table exist in a column of another table.

Here is an example of defining a FOREIGN KEY constraint in a table creation statement:

```
CREATE TABLE students (
    id serial PRIMARY KEY,
    name varchar,
    age integer,
    class_id integer REFERENCES classes(id)
);

CREATE TABLE classes (
    id serial PRIMARY KEY,
    name varchar
);
```

In this example, the "class_id" column in the "students" table has a FOREIGN KEY constraint that references the "id" column in the "classes" table.

5. CHECK Constraint: The CHECK constraint is used to limit the values that can be inserted into a column. It allows creating complex logical expressions to restrict the values of the column.

Here is an example of defining a CHECK constraint in a table creation statement:

```
CREATE TABLE students (
    id serial PRIMARY KEY,
    name varchar,
    age integer,
    class varchar,
    CONSTRAINT check_age CHECK (age > 10 AND age < 18)
);
```

In this example, the "check_age" constraint is defined to restrict the age value to be between 10 and 18.

Constraints are essential for maintaining data integrity in a database. They help ensure that only valid data is inserted into a table and prevent data inconsistencies that can lead to data corruption or incorrect results in queries. By enforcing constraints, the database system provides a reliable and consistent data store for your application.

3.12   How do you use the EXPLAIN and EXPLAIN ANALYZE commands to analyze query performance in PostgreSQL?

The EXPLAIN and EXPLAIN ANALYZE commands are powerful tools for analyzing query performance in PostgreSQL.

EXPLAIN will show the plan that the PostgreSQL planner generated for a SQL statement while EXPLAIN ANALYZE will show the same plan but also execute the query and display actual runtimes and row counts.

To use EXPLAIN, simply prepend the SQL statement with the keyword EXPLAIN, like this:

```
EXPLAIN SELECT * FROM mytable WHERE id = 10;
```

This will output the execution plan for the query. The output consists of a tree of nodes, with each node representing an operation in the plan. The nodes are indented to show the hierarchical structure of the plan.

Heres an example output:

```
                    QUERY PLAN
-------------------------------------------------------
 Seq Scan on mytable  (cost=0.00..12.50 rows=1 width=62)
   Filter: (id = 10)
```

The output gives us important information about the plan. In this case, the query uses a sequential scan on the 'mytable' table and applies a filter for 'id = 10'. The 'cost' field represents the estimated cost of each operation in the plan. Lower costs indicate faster operations.

EXPLAIN ANALYZE is used in the same way as EXPLAIN, but it also executes the query and shows actual runtimes and row counts. Heres an example:

```
EXPLAIN ANALYZE SELECT * FROM mytable WHERE id = 10;
```

The output will be similar to EXPLAIN's, but it will include runtimes and row counts for each node in the plan.

```
QUERY PLAN
------------------------------------------------------------
 Seq Scan on mytable (cost=0.00..12.50 rows=1 width=62) (actual time
     =0.015..0.015 rows=1 loops=1)
   Filter: (id = 10)
   Rows Removed by Filter: 999
 Planning time: 0.086 ms
 Execution time: 0.042 ms
```

The 'actual time' field represents the actual time taken by each operation in the plan. The 'loops' field represents the number of times the operation was executed. The 'Rows Removed by Filter' field shows how many rows were filtered out by the WHERE clause.

In conclusion, EXPLAIN and EXPLAIN ANALYZE commands in PostgreSQL are useful tools for analyzing and optimizing query performance. By examining the query execution plan and collecting actual runtime statistics, you can identify slow-performing queries and improve them.

3.13   What is the difference between a full-text search and a LIKE query in PostgreSQL, and when should you use each?

A full-text search and a 'LIKE' query are both used for searching data in a PostgreSQL database, but there are some key differences between them.

A 'LIKE' query matches a pattern against a text string, returning all rows where the column value satisfies the pattern. The pattern can use the '%' wildcard character to match zero or more characters, and the '_' wildcard character to match any single character. For example:

```
String searchTerm = "apple";
String query = "SELECT * FROM products WHERE name LIKE '%" + searchTerm + "%'
      ";
```

This query will find all products with a name containing the word "apple", such as "Apple iPhone" or "Red Delicious Apples".

On the other hand, a full-text search performs a linguistic search against document data, looking for matches based on the meaning of the words in the data. It takes into account synonyms, stemming (reducing words to their root form), and other language-specific rules. To perform a full-text search in PostgreSQL, you need to create a text search index and use the 'tsvector' data type to represent the indexed columns. For example:

```
String searchTerm = "apple";
String query = "SELECT␣*␣FROM␣products␣WHERE␣to_tsvector('english',␣name)␣@@␣
    to_tsquery('" + searchTerm + "')"
```

This query will find products that contain the word "apple" or a semantically equivalent term, such as "apples" or "fruit".

So, when should you use a 'LIKE' query versus a full-text search? If you need a simple search for exact matches or partial matches based on simple wildcard patterns, a 'LIKE' query may be sufficient. For example, if you are searching for a specific word or phrase within a column, a 'LIKE' query may be the better option.

However, if you need to perform more complex searches that take into account linguistic rules and synonyms, a full-text search is likely the better option. Full-text search is particularly useful for searching large bodies of text, such as books or articles, where you need to find all relevant results based on meaning rather than just exact keyword matches.

3.14   How do you work with arrays and JSON data types in PostgreSQL?

PostgreSQL provides support for both arrays and the JSON data type. Here's how to work with them:

1. Arrays: Arrays are an ordered collection of elements of the same data type. In order to use arrays, you'll need to create a table with a column of type array. Here's an example:

```
CREATE TABLE my_table (
```

```
  id SERIAL PRIMARY KEY,
  values INTEGER[]
);
```

To insert data into the array column, you can use the array construc-
tor syntax:

```
INSERT INTO my_table (values) VALUES (ARRAY[1, 2, 3]);
```

To access the data in the array, you can use the array subscript syntax:

```
SELECT values[1], values[2], values[3] FROM my_table;
```

This will return the values 1, 2, and 3.

2. JSON data types: JSON data types allow you to store and manipulate JSON data within PostgreSQL. In order to use JSON data
types, you'll need to create a table with a column of type JSON.
Here's an example:

```
CREATE TABLE my_table (
  id SERIAL PRIMARY KEY,
  data JSON
);
```

To insert data into the JSON column, you can use the JSON syntax:

```
INSERT INTO my_table (data) VALUES ('{"name": "John", "age": 35}');
```

To access the data in the JSON column, you can use the JSON functions provided by PostgreSQL. For example, the following query will
return the value of the name property in the JSON data:

```
SELECT data ->> 'name' FROM my_table;
```

This will return the value "John".

You can also use the JSONB data type which provide improved indexing capabilities and reduced storage space comparing to the JSON
data type but require more processing power.

3.15   What are some performance tuning techniques you can apply to optimize PostgreSQL database performance?

There are several performance tuning techniques that can be applied to optimize PostgreSQL database performance. Some of the most effective ones are outlined below:

1. Indexing: Database indexing is one of the most effective ways to improve query performance. Proper indexing can improve query execution time by several orders of magnitude. Indexes help to speed up search operations by providing faster access to data. PostgreSQL provides several types of indexes including B-tree, hash, GIN, GiST, and SP-GiST indexes.

```
//Example of creating an index on a table column using Java and JDBC
Connection con = DriverManager.getConnection(jdbcUrl, user, pass);
Statement stmt = con.createStatement();
stmt.executeUpdate("CREATE INDEX idx_name ON table_name (name)");
stmt.close();
con.close();
```

2. Partitioning: Partitioning is a technique that involves dividing a large table into smaller and more manageable partitions. This can significantly improve query performance by enabling the database to access the required data more quickly. PostgreSQL supports both range and hash partitioning.

```
//Example of creating a partitioned table in PostgreSQL using Java and JDBC
Connection con = DriverManager.getConnection(jdbcUrl, user, pass);
Statement stmt = con.createStatement();
stmt.executeUpdate("CREATE TABLE measurement (ts timestamp, val double
    precision) PARTITION BY RANGE (ts)");
stmt.executeUpdate("CREATE TABLE measurement_y2016m01 PARTITION OF
    measurement FOR VALUES FROM ('2016-01-01') TO ('2016-02-01')");
stmt.executeUpdate("CREATE TABLE measurement_y2016m02 PARTITION OF
    measurement FOR VALUES FROM ('2016-02-01') TO ('2016-03-01')");
stmt.close();
con.close();
```

3. Connection pooling: Connection pooling is a technique used to enhance database performance by minimizing the time required to establish database connections. Rather than creating a new connection for each request, connection pooling reuses established connections.

```
//Example of using HikariCP to implement connection pooling in Java
HikariConfig config = new HikariConfig();
```

```
config.setJdbcUrl(jdbcUrl);
config.setUsername(user);
config.setPassword(pass);
config.setMaximumPoolSize(10); // Maximum number of connections in the pool
HikariDataSource ds = new HikariDataSource(config);
Connection con = ds.getConnection();
Statement stmt = con.createStatement();
// Perform database operations
stmt.close();
con.close();
ds.close();
```

4. Query optimization: Query optimization is a technique that involves analyzing and optimizing SQL queries to improve their execution time. This involves understanding the database schema and using proper query techniques such as joining tables and using subqueries.

```
//Example of using a subquery in a SQL query in Java
String query = "SELECT * FROM table1 WHERE id IN (SELECT table1_id FROM
    table2 WHERE condition = true)";
Connection con = DriverManager.getConnection(jdbcUrl, user, pass);
Statement stmt = con.createStatement();
ResultSet rs = stmt.executeQuery(query);
// Process the result set
rs.close();
stmt.close();
con.close();
```

5. Memory allocation: PostgreSQL performance can be greatly enhanced by ensuring that enough memory is allocated to the database. This means allocating memory properly for shared buffers, work_mem, maintenance_work_mem, and effective_cache_size.

```
//Example of setting the shared buffers and work_mem parameters in PostgreSQL
    using Java and JDBC
Connection con = DriverManager.getConnection(jdbcUrl, user, pass);
Statement stmt = con.createStatement();
stmt.executeUpdate("ALTER SYSTEM SET shared_buffers = '1GB'");
stmt.executeUpdate("ALTER SYSTEM SET work_mem = '64MB'");
stmt.close();
con.close();
```

These are just a few techniques that can be used to optimize PostgreSQL database performance. Other techniques include vacuuming, analyzing statistics, and optimizing disk I/O.

3.16 How do you manage user roles and permissions in PostgreSQL?

In PostgreSQL, user roles and permissions are managed using the role-based access control (RBAC) system. The RBAC system allows you to define roles and assign permissions to those roles, and then assign those roles to users.

Here's a brief overview of the steps involved:

1. Create roles: Use the 'CREATE ROLE' command to create roles in PostgreSQL. A role can be either a database user or a group of users. For example, to create a role for a database user, you can use the following command:

```
CREATE ROLE myuser LOGIN PASSWORD 'mypassword';
```

This creates a new role named 'myuser' with a login capability and a password.

2. Grant permissions to roles: Use the 'GRANT' command to grant permissions to roles in PostgreSQL. For example, to grant 'SELECT' permission on a table to a role, you can use the following command:

```
GRANT SELECT ON mytable TO myrole;
```

This grants the 'SELECT' permission on the 'mytable' table to the 'myrole' role.

3. Assign roles to users: Use the 'ALTER USER' or 'ALTER ROLE' command to assign roles to users in PostgreSQL. For example, to assign the 'myrole' role to the 'myuser' user, you can use the following command:

```
ALTER USER myuser WITH ROLE myrole;
```

This assigns the 'myrole' role to the 'myuser' user.

You can also use the 'REVOKE' command to revoke permissions from roles and the 'DROP ROLE' command to delete roles.

Here's an example Java code snippet that demonstrates how to create a role in PostgreSQL:

```java
import java.sql.*;

public class PostgresExample {
  public static void main(String[] args) {
    Connection conn = null;
    Statement stmt = null;
    String role = "myuser";
    String password = "mypassword";
    String createRoleSQL = "CREATE ROLE " + role + " LOGIN PASSWORD '" +
        password + "';";

    try {
      conn = DriverManager.getConnection("jdbc:postgresql://localhost/
          mydatabase", "myusername", "mypassword");
      stmt = conn.createStatement();
      stmt.execute(createRoleSQL);
      System.out.println("Role created successfully");
    } catch (SQLException e) {
      System.out.println("Error creating role: " + e.getMessage());
    } finally {
      try {
        if (stmt != null) stmt.close();
        if (conn != null) conn.close();
      } catch (SQLException e) {
        System.out.println("Error closing connection: " + e.getMessage());
      }
    }
  }
}
```

This code creates a new role named 'myuser' with a login capability and a password in the 'mydatabase' database. Note that you need to replace 'myusername' and 'mypassword' with your PostgreSQL username and password.

3.17   Explain the concept of table partitioning in PostgreSQL and its benefits.

Table partitioning in PostgreSQL involves splitting up a single large table into smaller, more manageable pieces called partitions. Each partition of the table contains a subset of the data based on specific criteria such as a range of values in a particular column or a particular value in a specific column.

Partitioning tables in PostgreSQL can provide several benefits, including:

1. Improved query performance: When working with very large tables, partitioning can improve query performance by reducing the number of records that need to be searched or accessed. Postgres can prune the partitions that do not need to be scanned, leading to significant performance improvements for queries that would otherwise scan the entire table.

2. Faster data loading and indexing: Loading data into a partitioned table can be faster than loading data into a non-partitioned table. Additionally, indexes can be created on individual partitions instead of the entire table, leading to faster indexing operations.

3. Efficient data management: Partitioning can make data management easier and more efficient, as administrators can manage each partition separately rather than needing to manipulate the entire table. For example, if some data needs to be deleted or archived, it can be done at the partition level. Additionally, backing up and restoring individual partitions is more straightforward than managing an entire table.

Heres an example of how to create a partitioned table in PostgreSQL using Java:

```
String createTable = "CREATE TABLE products (product_id INT, product_name
    VARCHAR, price DECIMAL(10,2), category VARCHAR, created_date DATE)";

String createPartitions = "CREATE TABLE products_y2000m01 PARTITION OF
    products FOR VALUES FROM ('2000-01-01') TO ('2000-02-01'), " +
                        "products_y2000m02 PARTITION OF products FOR VALUES
                            FROM ('2000-02-01') TO ('2000-03-01'), " +
                        "products_y2000m03 PARTITION OF products FOR VALUES
                            FROM ('2000-03-01') TO ('2000-04-01'), " +
                        "products_y2000m04 PARTITION OF products FOR VALUES
                            FROM ('2000-04-01') TO ('2000-05-01')";

Statement stmt = conn.createStatement();
stmt.executeUpdate(createTable);
stmt.executeUpdate(createPartitions);
```

In this example, we create a 'products' table with columns 'product_id', 'product_name', 'price', 'category', and 'created_date'. We then create four partitions 'products_y2000m01', 'products_y2000m02', 'products_y2000m03', and 'products_y2000m04' and assign data ranges to each partition based on the 'created_date' column. Any queries that filter on the 'created_date' column will be significantly faster because Postgres will only scan the relevant partition(s).

3.18   What are some common database maintenance tasks that a PostgreSQL DBA should perform?

Here are some common database maintenance tasks that a Post-greSQL DBA should perform:

1. Backup and Recovery: Regular backups are essential to ensure data is not lost due to system failures or errors. The backup should be tested periodically to ensure its integrity.

Example Java code for backup:

```
Process p = Runtime.getRuntime().exec("/usr/bin/pg_dump␣-U␣postgres␣-d␣mydb␣>
    ␣/path/to/backup/file/mydb.sql");
p.waitFor();
int exitValue = p.exitValue();
```

2. Monitoring: Monitoring the health of the database by checking system resources, database size, index usage, and queries that may be causing performance issues.

Example Java code for monitoring:

```
Connection conn = DriverManager.getConnection("jdbc:postgresql://localhost
    :5432/mydb", "postgres", "password");
Statement stmt = conn.createStatement();
ResultSet rs = stmt.executeQuery("SELECT␣*␣FROM␣pg_stat_activity");
while(rs.next()) {
    // process results
}
```

3. Index Maintenance: Regularly analyze and rebuild indexes to improve performance.

Example SQL code for index maintenance:

```
ANALYZE tablename;
REINDEX TABLE tablename;
```

4. Vacuuming: Regularly vacuum the database to free up unused space and improve performance.

Example SQL code for vacuuming:

```
VACUUM VERBOSE tablename;
```

5. Performance Tuning: Analyzing queries and optimizing them for better performance.

Example Java code for performance tuning:

```
PreparedStatement pstmt = conn.prepareStatement("SELECT␣*␣FROM␣mytable␣WHERE␣
    mycolumn␣=␣?");
pstmt.setString(1, "myvalue");
ResultSet rs = pstmt.executeQuery();
while(rs.next()) {
    // process results
}
```

These are some common database maintenance tasks that a PostgreSQL DBA should perform to keep the database healthy and performant.

3.19 How do you use window functions in PostgreSQL, and what are their advantages?

A window function in PostgreSQL calculates a value for each row in a result set based on a window of rows. The window function is applied after the WHERE, GROUP BY, and HAVING clauses and before the ORDER BY and LIMIT clauses.

To use a window function in PostgreSQL, you need to define the window using the OVER() clause. The window can be defined to include a range of rows based on their position relative to the current row, or it can be defined to include all of the rows in the result set.

Here is an example of a simple window function that calculates a moving average for a set of numbers using the average of the three values before and after each row:

```
SELECT value, AVG(value) OVER (ORDER BY id ROWS BETWEEN 3 PRECEDING AND 3
    FOLLOWING) AS moving_avg
FROM mytable;
```

In this example, the window is defined to include the current row and the three rows before and after it, and the moving_avg is calculated for each row based on the values in this window.

Some advantages of using window functions in PostgreSQL include:

1. Simplified and more efficient queries: Window functions can simplify complex queries by eliminating the need for self-joins, subqueries, or temporary tables to calculate aggregate values. They also typically perform better than these alternative methods.

2. Ability to calculate rankings and percentiles: Window functions can be used to calculate rankings or percentiles based on a specific field or combination of fields. This is useful in analytical applications, such as financial analysis or marketing analysis.

3. More advanced analytics functionality: Window functions can be combined with other advanced analytics functions, such as the LEAD and LAG functions, to provide even more advanced functionality.

Overall, window functions are a powerful tool for performing advanced analytics and simplifying SQL queries in PostgreSQL.

3.20   What is the purpose of the .pgpass file, and how do you use it to securely store PostgreSQL passwords?

The .pgpass file is a plain text file that allows PostgreSQL users to securely store their passwords, and avoid the need to enter them manually every time they connect to a PostgreSQL instance. This file is particularly useful for scripting and automation tasks, as well as for interactive use.

The .pgpass file contains one entry per line, with fields separated by colons. The fields represent, in order: the hostname, the port number, the database name, the username, and the password. Each field can be replaced with an asterisk (*) to match any value. Comments can be added by prefixing a line with the hash symbol (#).

To use the .pgpass file, the file permissions must be set to 0600 (read-/write only for the owner), as the file contains sensitive information. When connecting to PostgreSQL, the client library (such as libpq in C, or the JDBC driver in Java) first checks if a .pgpass file exists in the user's home directory. If it does, it reads the file and attempts to match the connection parameters with each entry in the file, in the order they appear. If a match is found, the corresponding password is used to authenticate the user.

Here is an example of a .pgpass file:

```
# This is a comment
localhost:5432:mydb:myuser:mypassword
*:5432:*:myotheruser:myotherpassword
```

In this example, the first line matches connections to localhost on port 5432, to the database "mydb", with the username "myuser". The corresponding password is "mypassword". The second line matches connections to any host on port 5432, to any database, with the username "myotheruser". The corresponding password is "myotherpassword".

In Java, to use the .pgpass file with the JDBC driver, you can set the "user" property to the desired username, and leave the "password" property unset or null. The driver will automatically look for a .pgpass file in the user's home directory and use it to authenticate the user. Here is an example:

```
import java.sql.*;

public class Example {
    public static void main(String[] args) throws SQLException {
        String url = "jdbc:postgresql://localhost/mydb";
        String user = "myuser";
        String password = null; // Use .pgpass file
        Connection conn = DriverManager.getConnection(url, user, password);
        // Use the connection
    }
}
```

Chapter 4

Advanced

4.1 What are the different types of indexes in PostgreSQL, and when should you use each one?

PostgreSQL supports different types of indexes, each with its unique strengths and usage scenarios. Here are some of the most common index types in PostgreSQL:

1. B-tree index - This is the default index in PostgreSQL and is suitable for most use cases. It is a balanced tree data structure that allows fast lookup, sorting, and range queries for data stored in a table. B-tree indexes work best for columns with high selectivity (i.e., columns that have a wide range of distinct values), and the data is frequently updated.

Example code:

```
CREATE INDEX btree_index ON table_name (column_name);
```

2. Hash index - Hash indexes are faster than B-tree indexes for exact match queries, but they are not suitable for range queries. This type of index is best suited for columns with a small number of distinct values.

Example code:

```
CREATE INDEX hash_index ON table_name USING hash (column_name);
```

3. GiST index - GiST (Generalized Search Tree) index is an extensible index that supports different types of data structures and search algorithms. It is useful for complex data types such as geometric shapes, geolocation data, and full-text search.

Example code:

```
CREATE INDEX gist_index ON table_name USING gist (column_name);
```

4. GIN index - GIN (Generalized Inverted Index) index is designed for use with composite types and supports fast search and partial match operations. It is useful for columns that contain arrays or JSON data.

Example code:

```
CREATE INDEX gin_index ON table_name USING gin (column_name);
```

5. BRIN index - BRIN (Block Range INdex) index is useful for large tables that are frequently updated by appending data. It divides data into blocks and stores the minimum and maximum values for each block, making it efficient to scan and filter large tables.

Example code:

```
CREATE INDEX brin_index ON table_name USING brin (column_name);
```

In conclusion, choosing the right index type depends on the use case and the data type being indexed. For a standard data table with an integer ID column, B-tree index is the default and most commonly used type. But for more complex data types, choosing the right index is crucial for better query performance.

4.2 Explain the role of the Query Planner and Query Optimizer in PostgreSQL's internal workings.

The query planner and query optimizer are key components of PostgreSQL's internal workings and play a critical role in making the database management system highly performant and efficient.

Query Planner:

The query planner is tasked with taking the SQL query entered by the user and generating an execution plan that describes how the query should be executed. The planner takes into account factors such as query complexity, table sizes, available indexes, and server resources to come up with the most efficient plan.

The query planner uses a cost-based approach, which means that it assigns a cost to each possible execution plan, and then selects the plan with the lowest cost. This is achieved by estimating the amount of system resources needed to execute each step of the plan, such as CPU usage, memory usage, and disk I/O.

For example, given the following query:

```
SELECT *
FROM users
WHERE age > 25 AND state = 'CA'
```

The planner would generate an execution plan that involves filtering the records in the 'users' table based on the 'age' and 'state' columns using an appropriate index, and then returning the resulting records to the user.

Query Optimizer:

Once the execution plan has been generated by the query planner, the query optimizer takes over and applies additional optimization techniques to further improve the performance of the query.

The optimizer performs a variety of tasks, such as analyzing join and filtering conditions, removing redundant operations, and reordering operations to minimize the amount of data that needs to be read from the disk.

For example, if the query involves joining two large tables, the optimizer may choose to perform a hash join rather than a nested loop join, as it would be faster and more efficient for the given data set.

Additionally, the optimizer can take advantage of statistics and histograms that are generated by the database to make more informed decisions about which execution plan will be the most efficient.

In summary, the query planner and query optimizer work together to generate and execute the most efficient execution plan for a given SQL query. This makes it possible for PostgreSQL to handle large and complex data sets with ease, and to provide users with fast and accurate results.

4.3   How do you monitor and manage the performance of PostgreSQL using tools like pg_stat_statements and pgBadger?

PostgreSQL provides several tools to monitor and manage the performance of a database, including pg_stat_statements and pgBadger.

pg_stat_statements:

'pg_stat_statements' is a module that provides detailed statistics about resource usage for each query executed in the database. It tracks duration, number of executions, and the number of rows returned by each query. These statistics can be used to identify slow queries and optimize them for better performance.

To enable 'pg_stat_statements', you need to add the following line to 'postgresql.conf':

```
shared_preload_libraries = 'pg_stat_statements'
```

Then, to use 'pg_stat_statements' in a query, you need to enable the extension in the current database:

```
CREATE EXTENSION pg_stat_statements;
```

Once enabled, you can query the 'pg_stat_statements' view to retrieve the statistics. For instance, you could use the following query to list the top 10 most time-consuming queries:

```
SELECT query, total_time
FROM pg_stat_statements
ORDER BY total_time DESC
LIMIT 10;
```

'pg_stat_statements' also provides other useful statistics, such as the number of times a query was executed, the number of rows returned, and the average duration of each execution.

pgBadger:

'pgBadger' is a log analyzer that generates reports from PostgreSQL log files. It provides detailed information about slow queries, errors, connections, and other events in the database.

To use pgBadger, you need to first enable logging in the PostgreSQL configuration file 'postgresql.conf'. For instance, you could add the following line to log all statements:

```
log_statement = 'all'
```

Then, you can run 'pgBadger' on the log file to generate a report. For instance, the following command generates an HTML report from the log file '/var/log/postgresql/postgresql.log' and saves it to the file 'report.html':

```
pgbadger /var/log/postgresql/postgresql.log -o report.html
```

The report provides detailed information about the queries executed in the database, including the number of executions, the average duration, the slowest queries, and the queries that produced errors.

Using both 'pg_stat_statements' and 'pgBadger' can provide a powerful combination for monitoring and managing the performance of PostgreSQL. For instance, you could use 'pg_stat_statements' to identify slow queries and then use 'pgBadger' to analyze the detailed log information for those queries to identify the cause of the slow performance.

4.4   Describe the process of setting up and configuring connection pooling in PostgreSQL using tools like PgBouncer or Pgpool-II.

Setting up and configuring connection pooling in PostgreSQL involves the following steps:

1. Install the connection pooling application: You can either use PgBouncer or Pgpool-II to implement connection pooling. You can install these applications on your system via the PostgreSQL repository or from the applications website.

2. Configure the connection pooling application After installing the pooling application, you will need to configure it to suit your needs. The configuration files for these applications are located in different directories. For example, the configuration file for PgBouncer is pg_bouncer.ini, while that for Pgpool-II is pgpool.conf.

3. Configure Postgres server Next, you need to configure the Postgres server to enable connection pooling. You do this by adjusting the max_connections parameter in the postgresql.conf file. This setting determines the maximum number of connections to the database that the server will allow at any time.

4. Start the connection pooling application After configuring the pooling application, you need to launch it. You can do this by invoking the command line tool for the application. Depending on the application, you may need to specify some options.

5. Modify your application Finally, you will need to modify your application to take advantage of the database pooling. If you are using Java, you can configure the JDBC driver to use the pooling application by specifying the appropriate URL. For example, if you are using PgBouncer, your JDBC URL might look like this:

jdbc:postgresql:pgbouncer://localhost/mydatabase

This URL tells the JDBC driver to communicate with the PgBouncer connection pooling application running on the local machine and connect to the mydatabase database.

In summary, configuring connection pooling in PostgreSQL involves installing and configuring the pooling application, setting up the Postgres server, starting the pooling application, and modifying your application to use the pooling application.

4.5 Explain the role of tablespaces in PostgreSQL and how they can be used for disk space management.

Tablespaces in PostgreSQL are used for managing the physical storage location of database objects such as tables, indexes, and system catalogs. They provide a way to organize the database objects across different storage locations, enabling database administrators to optimize performance and efficiently utilize disk space.

In PostgreSQL, tablespaces are created using the 'CREATE TABLESPACE' command, specifying the name of the tablespace, its physical location on the file system, and any optional parameters such as the block size and file system permissions. Here is an example of creating a tablespace:

```
CREATE TABLESPACE mytablespace LOCATION '/path/to/mytablespace';
```

When a table or index is created with a specific tablespace, it will be physically located in that tablespace's storage location. For example, the following 'CREATE TABLE' statement creates a table named 'mytable' in the 'mytablespace' tablespace:

```
CREATE TABLE mytable (id SERIAL, name VARCHAR(50)) TABLESPACE mytablespace;
```

Tablespaces can also be used for disk space management. For instance, if a table or index grows too large and starts to cause performance issues or take up too much space on the current disk, it can be moved to a different tablespace located on a different disk or even a different machine. This can be done using the 'ALTER TABLE' command with the 'SET TABLESPACE' option, as follows:

```
ALTER TABLE mytable SET TABLESPACE mynewtablespace;
```

In addition, tablespaces can be used for backup and disaster recovery strategies. By storing different tablespaces on different disks or machines, backups can be taken more efficiently, and disaster recovery plans can be more effectively implemented.

In conclusion, tablespaces are an essential feature of PostgreSQL that allow for efficient disk space management, optimal performance, backup and disaster recovery strategies, and general database organization.

4.6   How do you perform point-in-time recovery (PITR) in PostgreSQL using WAL archives and base backups?

Performing point-in-time recovery (PITR) in PostgreSQL involves restoring a database to a specific point in time using a combination of base backups and Write-Ahead Log (WAL) archives. This process is useful in case data has been accidentally deleted or a database has become corrupt, and you need to restore it to a specific point in time, equal to or earlier than the last transaction committed to the database. To perform PITR in PostgreSQL, you will follow these steps:

1. Set up WAL archiving in the PostgreSQL configuration file. This will allow PostgreSQL to store transaction log files in a specific directory as they are being written. You can do this by editing the 'postgresql.conf' file and setting the following parameters:

```
wal_level = replica
archive_mode = on
archive_command = 'cp␣%p␣/path/to/wal/archive/%f'
```

This configuration will ensure that all WAL files are copied to the specified directory for archiving.

2. Create a base backup of the database. This is a complete backup of the database files, including all data and metadata at a specific point in time. To create a base backup, you can use the 'pg_basebackup' utility, as shown in the following Java code:

```
String backupDir = "/path/to/backup/dir";
String dbHost = "localhost";
String dbPort = "5432";
String dbName = "mydb";
String user = "myuser";
String[] pgBaseBackupCmd = new String[] {
    "pg_basebackup",
    "-h", dbHost,
    "-p", dbPort,
    "-U", user,
    "-D", backupDir,
    "-Ft",
    "-z"
};
ProcessBuilder pb = new ProcessBuilder(pgBaseBackupCmd);
Process p = pb.start();
int exitCode = p.waitFor();
```

This code will create a base backup in the specified directory in a compressed tar archive format.

3. Create a recovery.conf file in the PostgreSQL data directory. This configuration file specifies the location of the WAL archives and the starting point for the recovery process. You can create a recovery.conf file with the following contents:

```
restore_command = 'cp /path/to/wal/archive/%f %p'
recovery_target_time = 'YYYY-MM-DD HH:MI:SS'
```

Replace 'YYYY-MM-DD HH:MI:SS' with the specific date and time to which you want to restore the database.

4. Start the PostgreSQL server in recovery mode. This will initiate the recovery process and apply all WAL files up to the specified point in time. You can do this using the following Java code:

```
String dataDir = "/path/to/postgres/data";
String[] pgCtlCmd = new String[] {
    "pg_ctl",
    "-D", dataDir,
    "start",
    "-w",
    "-t", "600",
    "-o", "-c"recovery_target_timeline='latest'""
};
ProcessBuilder pb = new ProcessBuilder(pgCtlCmd);
Process p = pb.start();
int exitCode = p.waitFor();
```

This code will start the PostgreSQL server in recovery mode and apply all WAL files up to the specified time.

5. Verify that the recovery process was successful. You can connect

to the PostgreSQL server using a database tool and execute queries to verify that the data has been restored to the specific point in time.

In conclusion, performing point-in-time recovery in PostgreSQL using WAL archives and base backups involves configuring WAL archiving, creating a base backup, creating a recovery.conf file, starting the PostgreSQL server in recovery mode, and verifying the recovery process.

4.7   What are the different isolation levels in PostgreSQL, and how do they affect transaction behavior and performance?

PostgreSQL supports four isolation levels defined by the SQL standard:

```
1. Read Uncommitted
2. Read Committed
3. Repeatable Read
4. Serializable
```

The lower isolation levels offer higher performance but less transactional safety, while the higher ones offer less performance but stronger guarantees.

1. **Read Uncommitted**: This isolation level allows a transaction to see uncommitted changes from other transactions. This means that dirty reads are possible, in which an uncommitted change can be read by another transaction, leading to inconsistent data. This is the lowest level of isolation and is not recommended for most applications.

2. **Read Committed**: In this isolation level, a transaction can only see committed changes from other transactions. A dirty read is not possible, as a transaction will only see changes that have been committed. However, non-repeatable reads may occur, in which a query may yield different results if it is run multiple times within the same transaction due to other transactions committing changes in the meantime.

3. **Repeatable Read**: In this isolation level, a transaction will

only see changes that were committed before it started. This means that a transaction will not see changes made by other transactions during its execution. This provides stronger guarantees than read committed, but can lead to phantom reads, in which a query yields different results when run multiple times within the same transaction due to other transactions inserting or deleting rows.

4. **Serializable**: This is the strongest isolation level, in which a transaction enforces that its execution should not conflict with the execution of any other transaction. This guarantees that a transaction will appear to be executing alone, and will not see changes made by other transactions or allow other transactions to see its changes until it commits. Serializable can lead to serialization failures, in which two transactions cannot execute concurrently due to conflicts, and one of them must be aborted and retried to avoid deadlocks.

Performance-wise, the lower isolation levels have lower overhead and are generally faster, as they allow for more concurrency between transactions. Serializable, on the other hand, has higher overhead due to the need for conflict detection and may lead to performance degradation under high concurrency. It is important to choose an appropriate isolation level based on the consistency and safety requirements of your application, balancing it with the desired performance characteristics.

In PostgreSQL, you can set the isolation level using the 'SET TRANSACTION' command, for example:

```
connection.setTransactionIsolation(Connection.TRANSACTION_READ_COMMITTED);
```

4.8 Explain the concept of full-text search in PostgreSQL, including text search functions, text search operators, and tsvector and tsquery data types.

Full-text search in PostgreSQL is a powerful tool for searching through text-heavy datasets. It allows you to perform complex searches that take into account the structure of text and the relationships between words.

Text search functions in PostgreSQL are used to manipulate text data
in various ways. These functions can be used to perform string manipulation, pattern matching, and text normalization. One example
of a text search function is the 'to_tsvector' function, which takes a
text string and produces a 'tsvector' value that can be used in full-text
searches.

Text search operators in PostgreSQL are used to perform comparisons
between text data. These operators can be used to check for equality,
inequality, or similarity between text values. For example, the '@@'
operator is used to perform full-text searches with the 'tsvector' and
'tsquery' data types.

The 'tsvector' data type is a text search document that stores a nor-
malized version of the text data along with position and weight information. This data type is used to index text data in PostgreSQL
to allow for fast full-text searches.

The 'tsquery' data type is used to specify search terms in a full-text
search. This data type allows for complex search queries that take
into account text structure and relationships between words.

Here's an example of using a full-text search in PostgreSQL with Java:

```
// Connect to the PostgreSQL database
Connection conn = DriverManager.getConnection(
    "jdbc:postgresql://localhost:5432/mydb", "postgres", "password");

// Create a prepared statement with a full-text search query
PreparedStatement stmt = conn.prepareStatement(
    "SELECT * FROM documents WHERE to_tsvector('english', content) @@
        to_tsquery(?)");

// Set the search query parameter
stmt.setString(1, "cat & dog");

// Execute the query
ResultSet rs = stmt.executeQuery();

// Process the results
while (rs.next()) {
    int id = rs.getInt("id");
    String title = rs.getString("title");
    String content = rs.getString("content");
    // Do something with the results
}

// Close the database connection
rs.close();
stmt.close();
conn.close();
```

In this example, we connect to a PostgreSQL database and create a prepared statement that performs a full-text search query using the 'to_tsvector' and 'to_tsquery' functions. We then set the search query parameter to '"cat & dog"', which searches for documents that contain both the words "cat" and "dog". Finally, we process the results and close the database connection.

Overall, full-text search in PostgreSQL provides a powerful and flexible way to search through text data. By using text search functions, text search operators, and the 'tsvector' and 'tsquery' data types, you can perform complex searches that are tailored to your specific needs.

4.9 How do you manage database schema migrations in PostgreSQL using tools like Flyway or Sqitch?

When it comes to managing database schema migrations in PostgreSQL, Flyway and Sqitch are two popular tools. Both tools are designed to manage database schema changes and help ensure that those changes are applied in a reliable and repeatable manner.

Flyway is a database migration tool that focuses on simplicity and ease-of-use. It is based on the idea of "database as code", where the database schema is treated as a codebase that can be version-controlled and managed using standard development tools. Flyway uses simple SQL scripts that are executed in a specific order to change the database schema.

Sqitch, on the other hand, is a "change management" tool that focuses on tracking changes to the database schema over time. It uses a combination of SQL scripts and metadata files to manage schema changes, and it provides a detailed audit trail of all changes made to the database over time.

Regardless of which tool you choose, the basic approach to managing database schema migrations using these tools is similar. Here are the general steps you should follow:

1. Set up the tool: Install Flyway or Sqitch on your machine, add the

necessary configuration files and scripts, and make sure everything is working correctly.

2. Create the migration scripts: Create SQL scripts that define the changes you want to make to the database schema. These scripts should include the necessary DDL statements to create, modify, or delete database objects.

3. Apply the migration scripts: Run the migration scripts in the order specified by the tool. This will apply the changes to the database schema.

4. Test the changes: Once the changes have been applied, test your application to ensure that everything is still working as expected.

5. Commit the migration: Once you are satisfied that the changes are working correctly, commit the migration to version control. This creates an audit trail of the changes that have been made to the database schema over time.

Here is an example of how you might use Flyway to manage database schema migrations in a Java application:

1. Set up Flyway

```
Flyway flyway = Flyway.configure()
    .dataSource("jdbc:postgresql://localhost:5432/mydb", "username", "password
        ")
    .locations("classpath:db/migration")
    .load();
```

2. Create the migration scripts

Create a new SQL script in
'src/main/resources/db/migration/V1___create_table.sql':

```
CREATE TABLE my_table (
    id SERIAL PRIMARY KEY,
    name VARCHAR(255) NOT NULL,
    email VARCHAR(255) NOT NULL
);
```

Create a new SQL script in
'src/main/resources/db/migration/V2___add_column_to_table.sql':

```
ALTER TABLE my_table ADD COLUMN created_at TIMESTAMP DEFAULT NOW();
```

3. Apply the migration scripts

```
flyway.migrate();
```

4. Test the changes

```
// Make sure the table and new column exist
Connection conn = dataSource.getConnection();
Statement stmt = conn.createStatement();
ResultSet rs = stmt.executeQuery("SELECT * FROM my_table");
while (rs.next()) {
  System.out.println(rs.getInt("id") + ", " + rs.getString("name") +
      ", " + rs.getString("email") + ", " + rs.getTimestamp("created_at"));
}
rs.close();
stmt.close();
conn.close();
```

5. Commit the migration

Commit the 'V1__create_table.sql' and 'V2__add_column_to_table.sql'
scripts to version control.

Overall, using a tool like Flyway or Sqitch can make managing database
schema migrations much easier and more reliable. These tools provide
a clear audit trail of changes made to the database schema, and they
make it easier to handle complex database changes and dependencies.

4.10   How do you use foreign data wrappers (FDWs) in PostgreSQL to query data from external sources like other databases or CSV files?

PostgreSQL provides the Foreign Data Wrapper (FDW) feature for
querying data from external sources like other databases or CSV files.
This feature allows you to connect to external data sources and access
them as if they are local PostgreSQL tables.

FDWs in PostgreSQL are implemented as extensions, so first, you
need to make sure that the required extension is installed. The following command can be used to install the extension for different
types of data sources:

```
CREATE EXTENSION IF NOT EXISTS postgres_fdw;
CREATE EXTENSION IF NOT EXISTS file_fdw;
CREATE EXTENSION IF NOT EXISTS mysql_fdw;
```

Once the extension is installed, you can create a foreign server that points to the external data source to be queried. For example, to create a foreign server that connects to a MySQL database, you can use the following SQL statement:

```
CREATE SERVER my_mysql_server
FOREIGN DATA WRAPPER mysql_fdw
OPTIONS (host 'localhost', port '3306', dbname 'mydatabase');
```

Next, you need to create a user mapping that specifies the credentials for accessing the external data source. For example, to create a user mapping for a MySQL database, you can use the following SQL statement:

```
CREATE USER MAPPING FOR postgres
SERVER my_mysql_server
OPTIONS (username 'myuser', password 'mypassword');
```

Once you have created the foreign server and user mapping, you can create a foreign table that represents the external data source. For example, to create a foreign table that represents a table in a MySQL database, you can use the following SQL statement:

```
CREATE FOREIGN TABLE mytable (
    id integer,
    name character varying(50),
    age integer
)
SERVER my_mysql_server
OPTIONS (schema_name 'mydatabase', table_name 'mytable');
```

You can then use standard SQL queries to query the foreign table just like you would any other PostgreSQL table. For example, to select all the rows from the foreign table, you can use the following SQL statement:

```
SELECT * FROM mytable;
```

FDWs can also be used to query data from CSV files. To do this, you need to create a foreign table that represents the CSV file. For example, to create a foreign table that represents a CSV file, you can use the following SQL statement:

```
CREATE FOREIGN TABLE mycsv (
    id integer,
    name character varying(50),
    age integer
)
SERVER file_server
OPTIONS (filename '/path/to/myfile.csv', format 'csv');
```

You can then use standard SQL queries to query the foreign table just like you would any other PostgreSQL table. For example, to select all the rows from the foreign table, you can use the following SQL statement:

```
SELECT * FROM mycsv;
```

FDWs provide a powerful mechanism for querying data from external sources in PostgreSQL.

4.11   What are the various options for sharding in PostgreSQL, and what are their trade-offs?

Sharding is an approach to horizontally partitioning large databases into smaller, more manageable pieces, and PostgreSQL offers several options that one can use for sharding purposes:

1. Built-in Partitioning: PostgreSQL offers native support for partitioning by range, list, or hash. Using the built-in partitioning feature, you can split a table into several smaller tables based on a specific criterion like date, region, tenant, or product. The primary advantage of built-in partitioning is ease of use; however, it comes with limitations. For example, a partitioned table can only be split among fixed partitions that are declared during table creation.

2. Table Inheritance: Table inheritance is another option for achieving sharding in PostgreSQL. Table inheritance is a mechanism that allows one to define a parent table and derive child tables that inherit all the fields and behavior of the parent. Table inheritance can be used to split a large table horizontally into smaller child tables based on different criteria such as customer, region, or date. In this approach, each child table has its underlying physical storage that

can be controlled and managed separately from the parent table. Table inheritance offers the advantage of more flexibility for sharding but has some limitations like slower query performance and increased complexity.

3. Citus Data: Citus is an extension of PostgreSQL that provides sharding capabilities. With Citus, the tables can be sharded across a cluster of servers. The data is distributed and replicated across the cluster in a way that allows queries to be executed across multiple nodes in the cluster. Citus offers the advantages of easier scalability, fault tolerance, and higher performance; however, it comes with added operational complexity for managing the distributed nodes.

4. Postgres-XL: Postgres-XL is another extension of PostgreSQL that offers sharding and other features such as distributed transactions, parallel queries, and declarative partitioning. PostgreSQL cluster breaks the database into smaller pieces spread across multiple nodes in a cluster. Each node contains a replica of a portion of the data, and queries are distributed across the nodes to improve performance. Postgres-XL offers the advantages of easy scalability, faster query processing, and fault tolerance for managing distributed database environments. However, the added operational complexity and the need for specialized database administration knowledge can be an issue.

All the above approaches have their benefits and limitations when it comes to sharding. The choice of the shard generation method depends on the application requirements, performance considerations, and operational considerations. Ultimately, understanding the trade-offs involved between the different approaches, implementing and testing their functionalities can help make an informed decision.

4.12   How do you use logical replication in PostgreSQL to replicate specific tables or schemas between databases?

Logical replication is a powerful feature introduced in PostgreSQL 10 that allows replicating specific tables or schemas between databases. It works by sending logical changes to a replication target rather than physical changes, which makes it more flexible and efficient than traditional physical replication methods.

To set up logical replication, follow these steps:

1. Enable logical replication on both the source and target databases by adding 'logical' to the 'wal_level' configuration parameter in 'postgresql.conf':

```
wal_level = logical
```

2. Create a replication slot on the source database using the 'pg_create_logical_replication_slot()' function. This will create a logical replication slot that the target database can use to receive changes:

```
Connection conn = DriverManager.getConnection("jdbc:postgresql://localhost
    :5432/source", "postgres", "password");
Statement stmt = conn.createStatement();
ResultSet rs = stmt.executeQuery("SELECT␣
    pg_create_logical_replication_slot('my_slot_name',␣'pgoutput');");
rs.next();
String slotName = rs.getString(1);
```

Note that the second parameter to 'pg_create_logical_replication_slot()' is the output plug-in. In this example, we're using 'pgoutput', which is the default built-in plug-in that produces a binary representation of the changes.

3. Configure the source database to replicate the tables or schemas you're interested in using a publication. A publication is a named set of tables or schemas that are replicated as a unit. You can create a publication using the 'CREATE PUBLICATION' SQL command:

```
Statement stmt = conn.createStatement();
stmt.execute("CREATE␣PUBLICATION␣my_publication␣FOR␣TABLE␣my_schema.
    my_table;");
```

4. On the target database, create a subscription to the publication on the source database using the 'CREATE SUBSCRIPTION' SQL command. Note that you'll need to supply the replication slot name you created in step 2:

```
Connection conn = DriverManager.getConnection("jdbc:postgresql://localhost
    :5432/target", "postgres", "password");
Statement stmt = conn.createStatement();
stmt.execute("CREATE␣SUBSCRIPTION␣my_subscription␣CONNECTION␣'host=
    localhost␣port=5432␣dbname=source␣user=postgres␣password=password'␣
    PUBLICATION␣my_publication␣WITH␣(slot_name␣=␣my_slot_name);");
```

The 'CONNECTION' option specifies the connection string and credentials for the source database, and the 'WITH' option specifies the replication slot name.

That's it! Once the subscription is created, the target database will begin receiving logical changes from the source database for the tables or schemas specified in the publication. You can monitor the replication progress using the 'pg_stat_replication' system catalog view.

4.13   What are some techniques to troubleshoot and resolve deadlocks in PostgreSQL?

Deadlocks occur in PostgreSQL when two or more transactions are waiting for locks that the other transaction holds. This results in a situation where none of the transactions can proceed, leading to a deadlock. PostgreSQL provides a few techniques that can be used to troubleshoot and resolve deadlocks:

1. Identify the source of the deadlock: First, it's important to identify the root cause of the deadlock. This can be done by reviewing the PostgreSQL server logs, specifically the deadlock detection messages that are generated when a deadlock is encountered. These messages provide information about the transactions involved in the deadlock and the specific objects they are trying to lock.

2. Analyze the queries involved in the deadlock: Once the source of the deadlock is identified, it's important to analyze the queries involved in the transactions. This can be done by reviewing the PostgreSQL statement logs to identify the specific SQL statements that are causing the deadlock. Additionally, it's useful to run an explain analyze on the queries to see if there are any inefficiencies that are contributing to the deadlock.

3. Adjust transaction isolation levels: Deadlocks can sometimes be the result of different transactions using different isolation levels. By adjusting the isolation level, it's possible to prevent deadlocks from occurring. For example, if two transactions are using the Serializable

isolation level, it may be helpful to switch to the Repeatable Read isolation level.

4. Increase available resources: Deadlocks can sometimes be caused by limited system resources. This can be addressed by increasing the available resources, for example, by adding more memory or increasing the number of available connections.

5. Implement locking strategies: PostgreSQL offers various locking strategies that can be used to prevent deadlocks. These include row-level locking and advisory locking. Row-level locking allows for finer-grained control over locks and can be used to reduce the likelihood of deadlocks. Advisory locking provides a way to temporarily reserve a resource to prevent other transactions from acquiring a similar lock, effectively preventing a deadlock.

Here's an example of how row-level locking can help prevent deadlocks:

```
// In transaction 1
BEGIN;
SELECT * FROM employees WHERE id = 1 FOR UPDATE;

// In transaction 2
BEGIN;
SELECT * FROM employees WHERE id = 2 FOR UPDATE;
UPDATE employees SET salary = 100000 WHERE id = 1;
COMMIT;

// Back in transaction 1
UPDATE employees SET salary = 80000 WHERE id = 1;
COMMIT;
```

In this example, if both transactions were trying to update the same employee record (i.e., both SELECT statements had the same employee ID), then a deadlock could occur. However, by using row-level locking (i.e., using FOR UPDATE), each transaction acquires a lock only on the specific record they are updating, preventing a possible deadlock.

4.14   Describe the role of the autovacuum process in PostgreSQL and how it affects performance and storage.

Autovacuum is an automatic maintenance process in PostgreSQL that helps to reclaim space and optimize performance by removing dead rows and defragmenting storage. It is responsible for cleaning up the bloated table data and also releases unused table space when users delete data.

PostgreSQL autovacuum consists of two processes: Autovacuum Worker and Autovacuum Launcher. Autovacuum Launcher process checks the PostgreSQL catalog for tables that need to be vacuumed or analyzed, then it sends a request to an Autovacuum Worker process to perform the task. Autovacuum Worker is responsible for performing the actual vacuuming and analyzing of tables.

The autovacuum process is important because it helps to maintain database health and improve query performance by keeping the required data on faster storage. If the autovacuum process is not running as expected, a database can become bloated with dead rows and indexes that slow down queries and degrade storage performance. Excess unoptimized data in the database can incur extra I/O, leading to slower response times and lower throughput.

When the autovacuum process runs, it creates new free space by removing dead rows, reducing the amount of storage required to store data in a database. This process helps to reclaim space that otherwise would have gone unused, and removes dead rows that may be occupying disk space without providing any value. By doing so, PostgreSQL can avoid the need to allocate new storage capacity, which results in cost savings and improved performance.

The autovacuum process has different parameters that can be set to modify the behavior of the process. These parameters control the scheduling of the autovacuum process, the aggressiveness of the data removal, and the amount of data analyzed during the vacuuming process. It is important to configure these parameters according to the workload of the database to ensure optimal performance and storage utilization.

Autovacuum can also have a negative impact on performance if it is not scheduled properly. Running the full autovacuum on large tables every time can impact database performance due to I/O and CPU utilization. Its important to find a balance between frequency and performance to ensure that autovacuum does not cause any performance degradation.

In summary, the autovacuum process plays an essential role in ensuring database health and optimizing performance by cleaning up bloat and reclaiming storage. Properly configuring the autovacuum parameters and scheduling ensure that the process runs effectively without impacting performance.

4.15 What is the concept of savepoints in PostgreSQL, and how can they be used in transaction management?

Savepoints in PostgreSQL allow you to set markers within a transaction, so that you can revert the transaction to a specific point if needed. This can be useful in situations where you need to roll back part of a transaction, without losing the work that was done previously in the same transaction.

When a savepoint is created, the current transaction state is saved to a named checkpoint. Later on, if it becomes necessary to roll back to that savepoint, the transaction can be rolled back to that specific point and all subsequent changes will be undone. PostgreSQL supports nested savepoints, which allows you to create multiple savepoints within a single transaction.

Here is an example of how to use savepoints in PostgreSQL from within a Java application:

```
Connection connection = null;
Savepoint savepoint = null;

try {
   connection = DriverManager.getConnection("jdbc:postgresql://localhost/
       mydatabase", "myuser", "mypassword");
   connection.setAutoCommit(false);

   // Perform some database operations
   somePreparedStatement.execute();
```

```
    // Set a savepoint
    savepoint = connection.setSavepoint("mySavepoint");

    // Perform some more database operations
    someOtherPreparedStatement.execute();

    // Roll back the transaction to the savepoint
    connection.rollback(savepoint);

    // Commit the transaction
    connection.commit();
} catch (SQLException e) {
    if (savepoint != null) {
        connection.rollback(savepoint);
    }
    connection.rollback();
    e.printStackTrace();
} finally {
    if (connection != null) {
        connection.setAutoCommit(true);
        connection.close();
    }
}
```

In this example, we start by creating a database connection and turning off auto-commit. We then perform some database operations, set a savepoint, perform some more database operations, and then optionally roll back to the savepoint. Finally, we commit the transaction or roll back completely if any error happened.

In summary, Savepoints in PostgreSQL provide a flexible way to handle transaction management by allowing you to selectively undo changes made within a transaction. This can be helpful in complex database operations where you need to manage your transaction state carefully.

4.16 How do you handle large objects (LOBs) in PostgreSQL, including BLOBs and CLOBs?

PostgreSQL has support for Large Objects, which are used to store binary and text data that is too large to be stored in a normal row. PostgreSQL Large Objects are implemented as a separate system object and are stored in a special area called the large object area. In PostgreSQL, Large Objects are represented by an oid value, which is a 4-byte unsigned integer.

To work with Large Objects in PostgreSQL, there are four main steps:

1. Create the Large Object: To create a Large Object, you need to open a connection to your database and then execute the 'lo_create()' function. The 'lo_create()' function returns the oid value of the new Large Object.

Here's an example of creating a new Large Object in Java:

```
Connection conn = DriverManager.getConnection(url, username, password);
int oid = LargeObjectManager.createLO(conn, LargeObjectManager.READWRITE);
```

2. Write Data to the Large Object: To write data to a Large Object, you need to open the Large Object for writing using the 'lo_open()' function. Once the Large Object is open for writing, you can write data to it using the 'lo_write()' function. When you're done writing data, you need to close the Large Object using the 'lo_close()' function.

Here's an example of writing data to a Large Object in Java:

```
// Open the Large Object for writing
LargeObjectManager lom = ((org.postgresql.PGConnection)conn).
    getLargeObjectAPI();
LargeObject lob = lom.open(oid, LargeObjectManager.WRITE);

// Write some data to the Large Object
lob.write("Hello,␣world!".getBytes());

// Close the Large Object
lob.close();
```

3. Read Data from the Large Object: To read data from a Large Object, you need to open the Large Object for reading using the 'lo_open()' function. Once the Large Object is open for reading, you can read data from it using the 'lo_read()' function. When you're done reading data, you need to close the Large Object using the 'lo_close()' function.

Here's an example of reading data from a Large Object in Java:

```
// Open the Large Object for reading
LargeObjectManager lom = ((org.postgresql.PGConnection)conn).
    getLargeObjectAPI();
LargeObject lob = lom.open(oid, LargeObjectManager.READ);

// Read some data from the Large Object
byte[] data = lob.read(1024);

// Close the Large Object
lob.close();
```

```
// Convert the data to a String
String strData = new String(data);
```

4. Delete the Large Object: To delete a Large Object, you need to open the Large Object for writing using the 'lo_open()' function and then call the 'lo_unlink()' function. Once you've unlinked the Large Object, you need to close it using the 'lo_close()' function.

Here's an example of deleting a Large Object in Java:

```
// Open the Large Object for writing
LargeObjectManager lom = ((org.postgresql.PGConnection)conn).
    getLargeObjectAPI();
LargeObject lob = lom.open(oid, LargeObjectManager.WRITE);

// Unlink the Large Object
lob.unlink();

// Close the Large Object
lob.close();
```

In summary, Large Objects in PostgreSQL are a powerful way to store binary and text data that is too large to be stored in a normal row. The Large Object API provides a simple and efficient way to work with Large Objects in your applications.

4.17   How do you use the NOTIFY and LISTEN features in PostgreSQL to implement publish-subscribe patterns?

The NOTIFY and LISTEN features in PostgreSQL can be used to implement a simple publish-subscribe messaging system. This feature allows PostgreSQL to proactively notify interested clients when certain events occur in the database. Here's how you can use PostgreSQL's NOTIFY and LISTEN features to implement a publish-subscribe pattern:

1. First, create a table where notifications will be sent. You could create a simple table named 'notifications' with a 'message' column:

```
CREATE TABLE notifications (
  message text
);
```

2. In the publisher (producer) application, use the 'NOTIFY' command to send a notification message to the database whenever a specific event occurs. For example, let's say you have an application that handles user registrations. Whenever a new user registers, a notification message is sent to the 'notifications' table:

```
try (Connection connection = DriverManager.getConnection(url, user,
        password);
    PreparedStatement statement = connection.prepareStatement(
        "INSERT␣INTO␣notifications␣(message)␣VALUES␣(?)");
    ) {
    // Perform user registration logic
    // ...

    // Send notification event to database
    statement.setString(1, "New␣user␣registered:␣" + username);
    statement.executeUpdate();

    // Cleanup resources
    // ...
}
```

3. In the subscriber (consumer) application, use the 'LISTEN' command to register interest in a specific notification event. The subscriber can then wait for incoming notifications using the 'PGConnection' interface's 'getNotifications()' method:

```
PGConnection connection = (PGConnection) DriverManager.getConnection(url,
        user, password);
connection.addNotificationListener((int processId, String channelName,
        String message) -> {
    System.out.println("Received␣notification␣on␣channel␣" + channelName +
        ":␣" + message);
});

connection.unwrap(BaseConnection.class).getNotifications();
```

4. Whenever the publisher's 'NOTIFY' command is called and a new event is broadcasted to the 'notifications' table, the 'addNotification-Listener' method in the subscriber's application will capture the event notification and print out the message.

This simple approach can be used to implement more complex publish-subscribe patterns by modifying the table schema, adding additional columns, and filtering events based on specific criteria.

4.18 Explain the difference between the Serializable and Snapshot Isolation levels in PostgreSQL, and their implications on transaction management.

The Serializable and Snapshot isolation levels are two different mechanisms for controlling concurrent access to data in PostgreSQL.

Serializable isolation level is the highest level of isolation in PostgreSQL, it guarantees that transactions behave as if they are the only ones operating on the data even though there might be multiple concurrent transactions. This means that transactions adhere to the Serializable isolation level standards, which will prevent any dirty reads, non-repeatable reads, and phantom reads. In Serializable isolation, after a transaction has acquired a lock on a row or table, it will hold it until the end of the transaction. This level is generally slow, so it should only be used when data integrity is most important.

Snapshot isolation level works differently from Serializable as it does not lock or block concurrent transactions. The Snapshot isolation level reads a consistent snapshot of the database at the beginning of a transaction and works on it during the transaction. This approach allows transactions to access the same database concurrently without blocking each other. Suppose a transaction tries to modify data that another transaction is also modifying, then PostgreSQL will detect the conflict and abort one of the transactions to prevent inconsistencies. This isolation level is much faster than Serializable and is suitable for use cases where data conflicts are unlikely.

Transaction management is a challenging issue to address with concurrent access in PostgreSQL. There are several considerations to be made when deciding which isolation level to use. Serializable provides a high level of security, but it can also result in blocking, causing slow transaction speeds. Snapshot isolation is non-blocking, faster, and suitable for scenarios with less contention.

Here is a Java code example that demonstrates the differences between the two isolation levels:

```
Connection conn = DriverManager.getConnection(url, props);
conn.setAutoCommit(false);
```

```
conn.setTransactionIsolation(Connection.TRANSACTION_SERIALIZABLE);

PreparedStatement pstmt = conn.prepareStatement(
    "SELECT * FROM accounts WHERE id = ?");
pstmt.setInt(1, 1);
ResultSet rs1 = pstmt.executeQuery();

// Transaction 1 holds a lock on the account with id=1.

PreparedStatement pstmt2 = conn.prepareStatement(
    "SELECT * FROM accounts WHERE id = ?");
pstmt2.setInt(1, 2);
ResultSet rs2 = pstmt2.executeQuery();

// Transaction 2 attempts to modify the account with id=2,
// but since transaction 1 is holding a lock, it is blocked.

// ... Do some work with the locked data ...

// The lock is released when the transaction ends:
conn.commit()


Connection conn = DriverManager.getConnection(url, props);
conn.setAutoCommit(false);
conn.setTransactionIsolation(Connection.TRANSACTION_SNAPSHOT);

PreparedStatement pstmt = conn.prepareStatement(
    "SELECT * FROM accounts WHERE id = ?");
pstmt.setInt(1, 1);
ResultSet rs1 = pstmt.executeQuery();

// Transaction 1 reads a consistent snapshot of the database.

PreparedStatement pstmt2 = conn.prepareStatement(
    "SELECT * FROM accounts WHERE id = ?");
pstmt2.setInt(1, 2);
ResultSet rs2 = pstmt2.executeQuery();

// Transaction 2 modifies another account, which does not conflict with
// transaction 1's snapshot, so no blocking occurs.

// ... Do some work with the modified data ...

conn.commit()
```

In summary, Serializable isolation is suitable for use cases where data integrity is critical, and Snapshot isolation is ideal for scenarios where data contention is minimal.

4.19   What are the various approaches for migrating data between PostgreSQL instances, such as logical backups, physical backups, and replication?

There are multiple ways to migrate data between PostgreSQL instances, and choosing the right approach depends on various factors such as the size of the database, the type of data being migrated, and the availability of network connectivity between the source and destination systems.

Here are three common approaches for migrating data between PostgreSQL instances:

1. Logical backups: In this approach, the data is exported from the source database instance using the 'pg_dump' utility, and then imported into the destination database instance using the 'pg_restore' utility. Logical backups are the most flexible and database-agnostic approach for migrating data, and they allow for granular control over the objects and data included in the backup. However, they can be slower and less efficient than other approaches, especially for large databases.

Here is an example of using 'pg_dump' and 'pg_restore' in Java:

```
// Export data from source database
ProcessBuilder pb = new ProcessBuilder("pg_dump", "-h", "source_host", "-U", "
    source_user", "-d", "source_db", "-F", "c", "-f", "backup_file.dump");
pb.start();

// Import data into destination database
ProcessBuilder pb2 = new ProcessBuilder("pg_restore", "-h", "dest_host", "-U",
    "dest_user", "-d", "dest_db", "backup_file.dump");
pb2.start();
```

2. Physical backups: In this approach, the data files are copied directly from the source database instance to the destination database instance using tools such as 'pg_basebackup'. Physical backups are faster and more efficient than logical backups, especially for large databases, but they require the destination system to have the same file system layout and hardware architecture as the source system.

Here is an example of using 'pg_basebackup' in Java:

```
// Create physical backup on source system
ProcessBuilder pb = new ProcessBuilder("pg_basebackup", "-h", "source_host", "
    -D", "/path/to/backup_dir", "-U", "source_user", "-F", "t");
pb.start();

// Copy backup to destination system
Files.copy(new File("/path/to/backup_dir").toPath(), new File("/path/to/
    destination_dir").toPath(), StandardCopyOption.REPLACE_EXISTING);
```

3. Replication: In this approach, the data is continuously replicated from the source database instance to the destination database instance using tools such as streaming replication or logical replication. Replication is the most efficient approach for migrating data, especially for large databases, and it can provide high availability and disaster recovery capabilities. However, it requires network connectivity between the source and destination systems, and it may introduce some overhead and complexity.

Here is an example of setting up streaming replication in Java:

```
// Configure source system to act as master
// (add these lines to postgresql.conf)
wal_level = replica
max_wal_senders = 5

// Create replication user on source system
CREATE USER replication_user REPLICATION LOGIN CONNECTION LIMIT 5 ENCRYPTED
    PASSWORD 'password';

// Start the replication process on destination system
ProcessBuilder pb = new ProcessBuilder("pg_basebackup", "-h", "source_host", "
    -D", "/path/to/destination_dir", "-U", "replication_user", "-X", "stream
    ");
pb.start();

// Set up replication connection on destination system
// (add these lines to recovery.conf)
standby_mode = on
primary_conninfo = 'host=source_host port=5432 user=replication_user password
    =password'
```

Keep in mind that these are just a few examples of the various approaches for migrating data between PostgreSQL instances, and there may be other tools and techniques available depending on your specific requirements and constraints.

4.20   How do you implement and manage high availability and failover solutions in PostgreSQL using tools like repmgr or Patroni?

High availability and failover solutions in PostgreSQL are essential to ensure data availability and reduce downtime. Two popular tools that can be used to implement and manage high availability and failover solutions in PostgreSQL are repmgr and Patroni.

Repmgr is a utility that simplifies the management of replication and failover. It can be used to set up replication between two or more PostgreSQL servers and facilitate failover when the primary server fails. Repmgr is designed to be used with streaming replication, which involves creating a standby server that continuously receives write-ahead logs (WAL) from the primary server. In the event of a failure, repmgr can automatically promote the standby server to be the new primary server, ensuring minimal downtime.

Patroni is a cluster manager that automates the management of PostgreSQL HA clusters. It uses leader election and consensus algorithms such as etcd or ZooKeeper to ensure the availability of the primary server. Patroni can also manage the creation of secondary replicas for load balancing and failover protection.

Here are the steps to implement and manage high availability and failover solutions in PostgreSQL using tools like repmgr or Patroni:

1. Install and configure repmgr or Patroni on all servers in the cluster.

2. Set up replication between the servers using streaming replication. In repmgr, this involves creating a standby server that follows the primary server. In Patroni, this involves creating a replica cluster that synchronizes with the primary server.

3. Configure repmgr or Patroni to monitor the status of the servers in the cluster. Both tools use a heartbeat mechanism to detect when a server has failed.

4. Set up automated failover in repmgr or Patroni. In repmgr, this

involves configuring a failover script that is executed when a server fails. The script should promote the standby server to become the new primary server. In Patroni, failover is automatic, and the tool handles the promotion of a secondary replica to the primary server.

5. Monitor the status and performance of the cluster regularly. This involves configuring alerts and monitoring tools to alert you when something goes wrong.

Here is an example of configuring repmgr in Java:

```
// Connect to the master server
Connection conn = DriverManager.getConnection("jdbc:postgresql://master:5432/
    mydb", "repuser", "password");

// Register the server in repmgr
RepmgrAdmin admin = new RepmgrAdmin(conn);
admin.registerNode("slave1", 5432, "/var/lib/pgsql/data");

// Create a standby server
RepmgrNode standby = admin.createStandby("slave1", "/var/lib/pgsql/data");

// Failover in the event of a primary server failure
RepmgrNode currentPrimary = admin.getPrimary();
if (!currentPrimary.isHealthy()) {
  RepmgrNode newPrimary = admin.promoteStandby(standby);
}
```

And here is an example of configuring Patroni in Java:

```
// Connect to the Consul service
Consul client = Consul.builder().build();

// Register the PostgreSQL service in Consul
Service service = ImmutableService.builder()
    .id("postgres")
    .name("postgres")
    .port(5432)
    .build();
client.agentClient().register(service);

// Configure Patroni to use Consul as the leader election service
Patroni patroni = Patroni.builder()
    .scope("my-cluster")
    .namespace("production")
    .postgresConfig("max_connections=100")
    .consulConfig(ImmutableConsulConfig.builder()
      .host("localhost")
      .port(8500)
      .build())
    .build();

// Start the Patroni cluster
patroni.start();
```

In summary, implementing and managing high availability and failover solutions in PostgreSQL involves setting up replication, monitoring

the status of the servers, and configuring automated failover. Both
repmgr and Patroni are popular tools for achieving these goals, and
they can be configured using Java or other programming languages.
Regular monitoring and testing are essential to ensure the availability
of the cluster and to minimize downtime.

Chapter 5

Expert

5.1 Describe PostgreSQL's internal architecture, including components like the parser, the planner/optimizer, and the executor.

PostgreSQL is based on a client/server model where a server process responds to requests from client programs. PostgreSQL is a multi-process system and it spawns a new process for each client connection. The server coordinates the activities of various internal components to manage data storage and retrieval.

Here is a high-level overview of the major components of PostgreSQL's internal architecture:

1. Parser: The parsing phase of a SQL query involves turning the string into a parse tree of tokens consisting of nodes like SELECT, INSERT, UPDATE, etc. The PostgreSQL parser reads the SQL input and produces an internal representation of the query in the form of a parse tree.

2. Planner/Optimizer: Once a parse tree for a query has been created, the planner analyzes it to determine how to execute the query.

The planner generates a query plan which involves selecting the best possible sequence of internal operations (such as table joins or index scans) to execute the query efficiently. The optimizer is responsible for selecting the most efficient plan given the available indexes and database statistics.

3. Executor: Once a query plan is generated and optimized, the executor component of PostgreSQL takes over. The executor performs the actual work of reading tables, performing joins, aggregating data etc. The executor interacts with the Operating System to read data from disk and write results back.

4. Storage Management: The storage management component of PostgreSQL is responsible for managing how data is stored on disk. It includes functionality for creating and managing tables, indexes, and other objects. PostgreSQL supports several storage management options, including row-based and column-based storage, which can be optimized for particular use cases.

5. Concurrency Control: Concurrency control is the component of PostgreSQL responsible for handling concurrent read and write operations. PostgreSQL uses a high-performance multi-version concurrency control (MVCC) system to provide concurrency control. This allows multiple transactions to read and write data at the same time, without locking tables or blocking other transactions.

6. Background Processes: PostgreSQL has several background processes that handle tasks like updating statistics, managing checkpoints and writing out data to disk. One of the most important processes is the WAL writer process which writes out transaction logs to disk. This ensures that data is recoverable in the event of a crash.

All of these components work together to provide a powerful and flexible relational database management system.

5.2 Explain how PostgreSQL uses write-ahead logging (WAL) for crash recovery and replication, and how it affects database performance.

PostgreSQL uses Write-Ahead Logging (WAL) to provide high availability, durability, and data consistency of the database in the event of a crash. WAL is a method of logging changes made to the database that ensures that the changes are written to the disk before the actual data is modified. This approach guarantees that even in the case of a sudden system failure, the database can be restored to a consistent state from the WAL.

WAL is also essential for replication, which is the process of copying data from one database to another. The WAL stream serves as the replication source, where the master node writes changes to the WAL log and the replica node reads them to apply it to its copy of the database.

The WAL process works as follows:

1. When a write operation is performed on the database, it is first written to the WAL log on disk.

2. After writing the information to the WAL, the modification can be applied to the actual database.

3. When the data is written to disk, PostgreSQL guarantees that it has been fully written and received its on-disk data pointer address.

4. WAL is continuously read from the log file and applied to the database periodically or in real-time, depending on the replication and crash recovery settings.

WAL provides several benefits for PostgreSQL, including:

1. Crash Recovery: WAL ensures the database can recover from unexpected shutdowns or hardware failures. During recovery, PostgreSQL reads the log to apply any changes that were not written to disk before the crash occurred.

2. High Availability and Durability: With the help of WAL, Post-greSQL can provide automatic failover and replication that guarantees data availability and durability.

3. Performance Impacts: WAL can negatively impact database write performance, especially for write-heavy workloads, as the log must be written to disk before the modification can be applied to the database.

Here is an example of implementing WAL in Java to replicate changes from one database to another:

```java
// create a PostgreSQL replication slot
ReplicationSlot slot = slotManager.create("logical_slot_name", "wal2json");

// get the changes from the WAL stream
try (WALStreamReader reader = new WALStreamReader(slot, lsrm, conn)) {
    while (true) {
        ByteBuffer msg = reader.read();
        if (msg == null) {
            break; // end of stream
        }
        // apply the changes to the target database
        applyChanges(msg);
    }
}
```

In this example, we create a logical replication slot on the master database and use WAL streaming to capture and replicate changes to the target database. The changes are read from the WAL stream as ByteBuffer messages and then applied to the target database.

5.3 How do you implement advanced monitoring and alerting for PostgreSQL using tools like Grafana, Prometheus, and Zabbix?

To begin with, Grafana, Prometheus, and Zabbix are popular open-source tools that can help monitor and alert you to issues with your PostgreSQL database. Here is how you can implement advanced monitoring and alerting using these tools:

1. Install and set up Grafana, Prometheus, and Zabbix: Firstly, you need to install and set up these tools. Grafana is used for visualization, while Prometheus is used for data collection and retention,

and Zabbix is used for alerting. Install these tools on a server or on multiple servers in a cluster.

2. Configure Prometheus to collect PostgreSQL metrics: Prometheus can collect PostgreSQL metrics using a PostgreSQL exporter. This exporter exposes PostgreSQL metrics via an HTTP endpoint, which Prometheus can scrape. In order to use PostgreSQL exporter, you need to install it on the database server, configure it to collect metrics, and then configure Prometheus to scrape those metrics.

Here is a sample Prometheus configuration to scrape PostgreSQL metrics from the exporter:

```
scrape_configs:
  - job_name: 'postgres-exporter'
    static_configs:
      - targets: ['postgres_exporter:9111']
```

3. Create Grafana dashboards: Once you've configured Prometheus to collect PostgreSQL metrics, the next step is to create Grafana dashboards to display the collected metrics. Grafana provides PostgreSQL-specific dashboard templates that you can use as a starting point for creating your own dashboards. These templates can be found in the Grafana dashboard repository.

4. Create Zabbix triggers: To be alerted of issues with your PostgreSQL database, you can use Zabbix triggers. A trigger is a condition that, when met, can activate an action, such as sending an email or a Slack notification. For example, you can create a trigger that alerts you when the number of active PostgreSQL connections exceeds a certain threshold.

Here is an example of a Zabbix trigger for active PostgreSQL connections:

```
{Template Postgresql:pg_stat_activity[application_name].num()}>{Template
    Postgresql:pg_settings[max_connections].last()}*0.9
```

5. Integrate Prometheus and Zabbix: Finally, you need to integrate Prometheus and Zabbix to enable alerting. Prometheus can send alerts to Zabbix using a webhook. You can configure Prometheus to send alerts to the Zabbix webhook when certain conditions are met, such as when the PostgreSQL connection count exceeds a certain threshold.

Here is an example of a Prometheus alert rule for PostgreSQL connection count:

```
groups:
- name: postgresql.rules
  rules:
  - alert: PostgreSQLConnectionCount
    expr: pg_stat_activity_count{state='active'} > 500
    for: 1m
    labels:
      severity: warning
    annotations:
      summary: "PostgreSQL connection count is high ({{ $value }})"
      description: "PostgreSQL connection count is currently {{ $value }},
        which is above the warning threshold of 500."
    receivers:
    - zabbix-webhook
```

With this configuration, when the PostgreSQL connection count exceeds the warning threshold of 500, Prometheus sends a webhook to Zabbix, which then triggers the alert, sending a notification to its configured channels.

Overall, implementing advanced monitoring and alerting for PostgreSQL requires setting up multiple tools and configuring them to work together. Once set up, these tools enable you to continuously monitor your PostgreSQL database and receive alerts when specific conditions are met, allowing you to proactively address issues before they cause problems.

5.4 Describe the process of tuning PostgreSQL's configuration settings, such as shared_buffers, work_mem, and maintenance_work_mem, for optimal performance.

Tuning PostgreSQL's configuration settings can significantly improve database performance. The following steps can guide you through the process of setting up PostgreSQL for optimal performance.

1. Identify the hardware: It is essential to understand the underlying hardware upon which the PostgreSQL database is running. Hardware information such as CPU speed, RAM size, storage configuration,

and disk I/O rates can help to determine the optimal PostgreSQL configuration to choose.

2. Identify the expected workload: How the database is used will impact the configuration of PostgreSQL settings. Workload information such as selectivity, complexity, query frequency, read-to-write ratio, etc., are needed to identify the appropriate settings.

3. Choose the appropriate settings: After identifying the hardware and expected workload, the appropriate configuration settings should be chosen. These settings include shared_buffers, work_mem, and maintenance_work among others. Below are some of the configuration settings and their optimal values:

- **shared_buffers:** This parameter determines the amount of memory dedicated to PostgreSQL to cache data pages. The optimal value for shared_buffers is approximately 25% of the available RAM on the database server.

- **work_mem:** This parameter sets the amount of RAM used by a sort operation for an individual session. The optimal value of work_mem can be determined by allocating 2% of the total RAM on the database server per session that performs sorting operations.

- **maintenance_work_mem:** This parameter sets the amount of RAM used for maintenance operations such as VACUUM, CREATE INDEX, etc. A useful rule of thumb when setting the maintenance_work_mem to use is allocating 25% of total RAM on the database server.

4. Measure and Monitor: To ensure that PostgreSQL is indeed optimized, it is essential to monitor the database through data logs, performance metrics, query logs, etc. Measuring and monitoring can help identify bottlenecks and challenges and adjust configurations settings.

5. Regular Review: Performance optimization is an ongoing process that requires regular reviews to be effective. With changes in workload, hardware, and other factors, PostgreSQL configuration settings will also need to be reviewed and adjusted to ensure optimal performance.

Example code in Java to modify the shared_buffers configuration setting:

```
Connection conn = DriverManager.getConnection(jdbc:postgresql://localhost/
    myschema?user=postgres&password=1234);
Statement stmt = conn.createStatement();
stmt.execute(ALTER SYSTEM SET shared_buffers=4GB);
stmt.close();
conn.close();
```

In this example, the shared_buffers setting is increased to 4GB. It is essential to note that changes to the PostgreSQL configuration require a PostgreSQL reload or restart to take effect.

5.5   How do you manage schema changes in a zero-downtime environment for PostgreSQL?

Managing schema changes in a zero-downtime environment for PostgreSQL involves careful planning, thorough testing, and implementation of proper techniques to ensure no downtime for users.

Here are some approaches that can be leveraged to achieve zero-downtime schema changes in PostgreSQL:

1. Online Schema Changes: One of the easiest ways to make schema changes is to employ the 'ALTER TABLE' command in PostgreSQL. However, the 'ALTER TABLE' statement acquires an exclusive lock on the table, which means other queries that try to access the table are blocked until the operation completes. To avoid this, we can use online schema change utilities like 'pg_repack', 'pglogical', and 'pg_bigm' to make non-blocking schema changes in PostgreSQL.

For example, we can use the 'pg_repack' tool to perform the online schema change of an existing index. The following Java code demonstrates how to perform 'pg_repack' operations using the 'ProcessBuilder' class:

```
ProcessBuilder pb = new ProcessBuilder("pg_repack", "table_name");
Process p = pb.start();
p.waitFor();
```

This will execute the 'pg_repack' command for the 'table_name' table and wait for the operation to complete.

2. Blue-Green Deployment: In a blue-green deployment model, we maintain two identical environments, one with the current schema version (blue) and the other with the modified schema version (green). We switch user traffic from the blue environment to green once all the schema changes are applied in the green environment. This approach eliminates downtime by ensuring that users always have access to a running system.

For example, we can have two PostgreSQL servers running in two different environments (e.g., blue and green). We can use a load balancer to route traffic to both these environments. Once we make schema changes in the green environment, we can switch user traffic from the blue environment to the green environment.

3. Multiple Versions of API: In this approach, we maintain multiple versions of the API that can serve requests of various schema versions. When we apply schema changes, we modify the latest API version to handle the new schema changes. This ensures that users who are using the latest API can perform database operations without any downtime, while users who are using an older version of the API may have limited access or experience gradual degradation.

For example, we can have two versions of our API, 'v1' and 'v2'. We can modify the 'v2' version to handle the new schema changes. Once the new schema changes are in place, we can gradually migrate users from the 'v1' version to the 'v2' version.

In conclusion, managing schema changes in a zero-downtime environment for PostgreSQL requires careful planning, thorough testing, and proper implementation of techniques like online schema changes, blue-green deployment, and multiple versions of the API.

5.6 Explain the concept of just-in-time (JIT) compilation in PostgreSQL and how it can improve query performance.

Just-in-time (JIT) compilation in PostgreSQL is a performance optimization technique where query execution plans are compiled at runtime, just before execution. In traditional ahead-of-time (AOT) compilation, the queries are compiled at the time of database creation or when new queries are added. However, with JIT, the compilation happens when the query is executed for the first time. This approach can improve query performance by reducing the overhead of repeated parsing and planning during query execution.

JIT compilation can be particularly useful in handling queries that have complex expressions or queries involving large data sets. For example, consider the following query:

```
SELECT SUM(price) + AVG(quantity) FROM sales WHERE sale_date BETWEEN '
    2020-01-01' AND '2020-12-31';
```

This query involves two functions, 'SUM()' and 'AVG()', and a range condition on the date. The query optimizer must first generate a plan that is tailored for this specific query, which involves parsing, analysis, and planning. JIT compilation can help optimize this process by compiling the plan before execution, so that the next time the query is executed, there is no need for parsing and planning.

In PostgreSQL, JIT compilation is enabled by default, but can be configured with different options to optimize queries based on the underlying hardware. For example, the 'jit_provider' configuration parameter can be set to the name of the provider for JIT compilation, such as LLVM or GCC. Additionally, the 'jit_above_cost' parameter determines at what cost a query will be compiled. Queries below this cost threshold will not be compiled, and will be executed normally.

Here is an example of using JIT compilation in Java using the JDBC API:

```
import java.sql.*;

public class JitDemo {
    public static void main(String[] args) {
        try (Connection connection = DriverManager.getConnection("jdbc:
            postgresql://localhost/mydb", "user", "password")) {
```

```
    try (Statement stmt = connection.createStatement()) {
        // Enable JIT compilation
        stmt.execute("SET jit = on;");

        ResultSet rs = stmt.executeQuery("SELECT * FROM mytable;");
        while (rs.next()) {
            // Process result set
        }
    }
} catch (SQLException e) {
    e.printStackTrace();
}
    }
}
```

In this example, the 'SET jit = on;' statement is executed before querying the database, which enables JIT compilation for subsequent queries executed by 'stmt'.

5.7 How do you use materialized views in PostgreSQL for complex query optimization and data warehousing scenarios?

Materialized views are a powerful PostgreSQL feature that enables users to store the result of a complex query as a precomputed table. This can be very useful in situations where the query takes a long time to run or when the data is being accessed frequently. Materialized views can help optimize complex queries and improve performance in data warehousing scenarios.

To create a materialized view in PostgreSQL, you can use the following syntax:

```
CREATE MATERIALIZED VIEW mv_name AS
SELECT column1, column2, ...
FROM table1
WHERE condition
GROUP BY column1, column2, ...
ORDER BY column1, column2, ...
```

Once the materialized view is created, you can refresh its data by running the following command:

```
REFRESH MATERIALIZED VIEW mv_name;
```

Here are a few examples of how materialized views can be used:

1. Complex Queries: Consider a scenario where you have a complex query that takes a long time to run because it involves multiple joins and aggregations. In this case, you can create a materialized view that precomputes the result of the query, and then use that view in subsequent queries instead of running the original query each time. This can significantly reduce the query execution time and improve performance.

```
CREATE MATERIALIZED VIEW complex_query AS
SELECT customer.name, SUM(order.amount) AS total_sales
FROM customer
JOIN order ON customer.id = order.customer_id
GROUP BY customer.name;
```

2. Data Warehousing: Materialized views can also be used for data warehousing scenarios where you need to store and analyze large amounts of data. In this case, you can create materialized views that aggregate and summarize the data, making it easier to query and analyze.

```
CREATE MATERIALIZED VIEW monthly_sales AS
SELECT date_trunc('month', order_date) as month, SUM(amount) as total_sales
FROM orders
GROUP BY month
ORDER BY month;
```

In conclusion, materialized views are a powerful feature in PostgreSQL that can be used to optimize complex queries and improve performance in data warehousing scenarios. They allow users to store precomputed results of a query as a table, which can be used in subsequent queries.

5.8 What are some advanced techniques for optimizing complex SQL queries in PostgreSQL, such as query refactoring, indexing strategies, and partitioning?

There are several advanced techniques for optimizing complex SQL queries in PostgreSQL. Here are some of them:

1. Query Refactoring:

Query refactoring refers to the process of rewriting a SQL query in such a way that its execution time is minimized, without changing its functionality. There are several techniques for query refactoring, such as:

- Subquery optimization: Subquery optimization involves breaking down a complex query into smaller, simpler subqueries that can be executed faster. For example:

```
SELECT * FROM orders WHERE customer_id IN (SELECT customer_id FROM customers
    WHERE last_name='Smith')
```

can be refactored as:

```
WITH smith_customers AS (
  SELECT customer_id FROM customers WHERE last_name='Smith'
)
SELECT * FROM orders WHERE customer_id IN (SELECT customer_id FROM
    smith_customers)
```

- Join optimization: Join optimization involves optimizing the join operations in a query to minimize the number of rows that need to be processed. For example:

```
SELECT * FROM orders INNER JOIN customers ON orders.customer_id=customers.
    customer_id WHERE customers.last_name='Smith'
```

can be refactored as:

```
SELECT * FROM orders WHERE customer_id IN (SELECT customer_id FROM customers
    WHERE last_name='Smith')
```

2. Indexing Strategies:

Indexing is a key technique for enhancing query performance by providing fast access to data. PostgreSQL offers several indexing strategies, such as:

- B-tree index: This is the most common index type in PostgreSQL, and it's useful for indexing columns that have low cardinality (i.e. fewer unique values).

- Hash index: This index type is useful for indexing columns that have high cardinality (i.e. many unique values), and it provides faster lookups than B-tree indexes for exact matches.

- GiST index: This index type is used for spatial data types, such as points, lines, and polygons.

- GIN index: This index type is used for full-text search, array, and JSON data types.

3. Partitioning:

Partitioning refers to the technique of dividing a large table into smaller, more manageable chunks called partitions. PostgreSQL supports several partitioning strategies, such as:

- Range partitioning: This involves partitioning the table based on a range of values in a certain column. For example, a table of sales orders could be partitioned by date ranges.

- Hash partitioning: This involves partitioning the table based on a hashing function applied to a certain column. This is useful for load balancing across multiple servers.

- List partitioning: This involves partitioning the table based on a list of discrete values in a certain column. For example, a table of blog posts could be partitioned by author.

Overall, optimizing complex SQL queries in PostgreSQL requires a combination of query refactoring, indexing strategies, and partitioning techniques, all of which should be carefully planned and implemented based on the specific needs of the application.

5.9 Discuss the implications of using different storage engines and filesystems with PostgreSQL, such as ZFS, XFS, and EXT4.

PostgreSQL is a powerful and flexible relational database management system that can be configured to work with different storage engines and filesystems to achieve various performance and reliability goals. In this answer, we'll discuss the implications of using different storage engines and filesystems with PostgreSQL, with a focus on ZFS, XFS, and EXT4.

Storage Engines:

PostgreSQL uses two main storage engines, namely writable and read-only storage. A write-ahead log (WAL) mechanism is used for handling the durable storage of transactional data. WAL enables fast transaction processing, disaster recovery, and replication. There are several storage engines that can be used with Postgres. Popular ones include:

1. PostgreSQL Native Storage Engine

The built-in storage engine is a row-oriented storage engine that is efficient for OLTP workloads. It can efficiently handle small to medium-sized databases. On-disk data storage requires a write-ahead log (WAL) mechanism to guarantee durability.

2. ZFS Storage Engine

ZFS is a popular storage engine that was designed specifically as a file system for use with databases such as Postgres. ZFS provides data compression, snapshots, and cloning, and copy-on-write capabilities, which results in significant disk space savings. It can be configured to provide high performance for large data workloads. ZFS also has built-in features for managing data duplication and data aging.

One of the benefits of using ZFS is that it provides excellent data integrity and self-healing capabilities. ZFS uses a copy-on-write (CoW) method, which means that blocks are never overwritten. And in the event of a disk failure or corruption, ZFS can detect and repair the problem without requiring a RAID system.

3. XFS Storage Engine

Also known as Extended File System, XFS is a high-performance file system that is used for large-scale, write-intensive workloads. XFS is ideal for databases that require high-speed writes and reads, as it supports file sizes of up to 16 exabytes, and it has support for parallel I/O.

If your use case requires a lot of read and write operations, then XFS may be the best option. One of the benefits of using XFS is that it performs well under heavy load and can handle a large number of small files.

4. EXT4 Storage Engine

EXT4 is a Linux filesystem that is widely used for storing data. It is optimized for high performance and provides features like journaling, file system-level encryption, and support for large files. It is a popular filesystem for Postgres, as it provides fast access to data and is very reliable.

One of the benefits of using the EXT4 buffer cache is that it is very efficient in managing system resources, which means that disk usage and resource allocation are optimized. Also, the EXT4 file system can be tuned for specific environments using mount options.

In summary, when selecting a storage engine, it is important to consider the required performance levels, the size of the database, and the type of workload. Choosing the right storage engine and tuning it correctly can greatly improve the performance of Postgres.

Filesystems:

Filesystems are responsible for storing and retrieving data on your computer. They are responsible for organizing data on the disk, managing file permissions, and ensuring the data is safe and secure. Different filesystems have different advantages and disadvantages.

1. ZFS Filesystem

ZFS is a file system that was designed for storing large amounts of data. It provides data compression, snapshots, and cloning, as well as copy-on-write capabilities. It is very reliable and provides excellent data integrity and self-healing capabilities. However, ZFS may require more system resources than other filesystems, which may be a drawback for some users.

2. XFS Filesystem

XFS is a high-performance filesystem that is designed for large-scale, write-intensive workloads. It is ideal for databases that require high-speed writes and reads, as it supports file sizes of up to 16 exabytes and has support for parallel I/O.

One of the benefits of XFS is its ability to handle metadata-intensive operations. Because of its advanced data structures, it can handle large numbers of files quickly and efficiently.

3. EXT4 Filesystem

EXT4 is the default filesystem for most Linux systems. It is optimized for high performance and provides features like journaling, file system-level encryption, and support for large files. It is a popular filesystem for Postgres, as it provides fast access to data and is very reliable.

One of the benefits of EXT4 is its ability to quickly access file metadata. The file system can also be tuned for specific environments using mount options.

In summary, choosing the right filesystem is important for Postgres performance. Each filesystem has its own advantages and disadvantages, and the choice will depend on the specific use case. When selecting a filesystem it is important to understand the workload and choose the filesystem that will best meet the needs of the database.

5.10 Describe the challenges and best practices for scaling PostgreSQL horizontally using sharding or partitioning solutions like Citus or PL/Proxy.

Scaling PostgreSQL horizontally using sharding or partitioning solutions like Citus or PL/Proxy can provide a lot of benefits, such as increased scalability, high availability, and improved performance. However, there are also several challenges that need to be considered along with the best practices to mitigate them.

Challenges:

1. Data Distribution: One of the biggest challenges when sharding is how to split the data among the shards. It is important to identify the right key to split the data based on the most common queries to ensure that the data is evenly distributed, and queries can be executed with minimum overhead.

2. Query Planning: When the data is split into multiple shards, query planning becomes a challenge as the query optimizer needs to consider the location of the data before calculating the optimal execution plan. As a result, the choice of a good sharding key is important to help the query planner make better decisions on optimizing the execution plan.

3. Distributed Joins: Distributed joins from tables in different shards can be expensive in terms of network overhead and query execution time. The decision on whether to use distributed join or move the data to a different shard should be considered based on the performance behavior of the dataset.

4. Data Consistency: In sharded databases, it is important to ensure the data consistency across shards. Inconsistent data can lead to unpredictable query results, application failures, or even data corruption.

5. Failover and Recovery: Failover and recovery have to be carefully planned and tested to minimize downtime and lost data.

Best Practices:

1. Design for Sharding: Design your data model to enable data to be split horizontally according to the distribution requirements. Identify the right sharding key that balances data distribution and query execution.

2. Monitor Performance: Monitor the performance of the individual shards to ensure the query loads are evenly distributed. If there is an imbalance, consider rebalancing the data.

3. Use a Connection Pooler: Use a connection pooler to manage connections to the individual shards. The connection pooler manages idle connections to ensure that the pool is always available for connections to the shards.

4. Use Distributed Transactions: Use distributed transactions to ensure data consistency across shards.

5. Test Failover and Recovery: Test the failover and recovery procedures to ensure that they are reliable and efficient.

Example Code:

Here is an example code for sharding a table using Citus:

1. Create a Citus cluster using Citus distribute table clause:

```
CREATE TABLE mytable (
  id bigint,
  name text,
  age integer,
  ...
) DISTRIBUTE BY HASH(id);
```

2. Insert data into the table:

```
INSERT INTO mytable (id, name, age, ...)
VALUES (1234, 'John Doe', 30, ...),
       (5678, 'Jane Doe', 25, ...),
       (9012, 'Bob Smith', 40, ...),
       ...
```

3. Query data from the table:

```
SELECT *
FROM mytable
WHERE id = 1234;
```

4. Join data from multiple shards:

```
SELECT *
FROM mytable
JOIN other_table ON mytable.id = other_table.mytable_id;
```

In the example code, the data is distributed based on the hash of the id column. Queries are executed on individual shards, and distributed joins are handled by Citus. Data consistency is maintained using distributed transactions. Failover and recovery are managed by Citus.

5.11   How do you implement advanced security features in PostgreSQL, such as transparent data encryption (TDE), data masking, and row-level security?

PostgreSQL provides various advanced security features to secure your data. Let's discuss each feature in detail:

1. Transparent Data Encryption (TDE):

Transparent Data Encryption (TDE) is a security feature that encrypts the entire database on disk. It ensures that even if someone gains access to your database files, they cannot read the data without the key to decrypt it. PostgreSQL does not have built-in TDE support, but it can be implemented using third-party extensions like PostgreSQL Transparent Data Encryption (PostgreSQL TDE) or pgcrypto.

Here's an example of how to use pgcrypto to encrypt a column:

```
import java.sql.*;
import org.postgresql.util.*;
...
// Establishing the connection
Connection conn = DriverManager.getConnection("jdbc:postgresql://localhost
    :5432/test", "postgres", "password");
// Enable pgcrypto extension
Statement stmt = conn.createStatement();
stmt.executeUpdate("CREATE EXTENSION IF NOT EXISTS pgcrypto;");
// Encrypting a column using pgcrypto
PreparedStatement ps = conn.prepareStatement("UPDATE users SET password =
    crypt(?, gen_salt('bf')) WHERE id = ?");
ps.setString(1, "myPassword123");
ps.setInt(2, 1);
```

```
ps.executeUpdate();
```

2. Data Masking:

Data Masking is a security feature that obfuscates sensitive data to protect it from unauthorized access. PostgreSQL does not have built-in data masking support, but it can be implemented using third-party extensions like Postgres Masking and Safeguard.

Here's an example of how to use Postgres Masking to mask a column:

```
import java.sql.*;
import de.zalando.pgobserver.msk.*;
...
// Establishing the connection
Connection conn = DriverManager.getConnection("jdbc:postgresql://localhost
    :5432/test", "postgres", "password");
// Enable Postgres Masking extension
Statement stmt = conn.createStatement();
stmt.executeUpdate("CREATE EXTENSION IF NOT EXISTS masking;");
// Masking a column using Postgres Masking
PreparedStatement ps = conn.prepareStatement("SELECT mask_email(email) FROM
    users WHERE id = ?");
ps.setInt(1, 1);
ResultSet rs = ps.executeQuery();
while (rs.next()) {
  System.out.println(rs.getString(1));
}
```

3. Row-Level Security:

Row-Level Security (RLS) is a security feature that restricts access to data at the row level. RLS ensures that only authorized users can view or modify selected rows in a table, based on predefined policies. RLS is built-in to PostgreSQL and can be implemented using policies defined in SQL statements.

Here's an example of how to use RLS to restrict access to a table:

```
import java.sql.*;
...
// Establishing the connection
Connection conn = DriverManager.getConnection("jdbc:postgresql://localhost
    :5432/test", "postgres", "password");
// Creating a table with RLS policy
Statement stmt = conn.createStatement();
stmt.executeUpdate("CREATE TABLE patients (id SERIAL PRIMARY KEY, name TEXT,
    ssn TEXT, doctor TEXT)");
stmt.executeUpdate("CREATE POLICY patients_policy ON patients TO doctors
    USING (doctor = session_user);");
// Inserting data into the table
PreparedStatement ps = conn.prepareStatement("INSERT INTO patients (name, ssn
    , doctor) VALUES (?, ?, ?)");
ps.setString(1, "John Smith");
```

```
ps.setString(2, "123-45-6789");
ps.setString(3, "Dr.␣Johnson");
ps.executeUpdate();
// Querying the table with RLS policy
ps = conn.prepareStatement("SELECT␣*␣FROM␣patients");
ResultSet rs = ps.executeQuery();
while (rs.next()) {
  System.out.println(rs.getInt(1) + "␣" + rs.getString(2) + "␣" + rs.getString
      (3) + "␣" + rs.getString(4));
}
```

5.12   Explain the concept of two-phase commit (2PC) in PostgreSQL and its role in distributed transactions.

Two-phase commit (2PC) is a protocol used in distributed transactions to ensure that any changes to data made across multiple systems are either committed or rolled back. In PostgreSQL, 2PC is implemented through the use of a coordinator process, which manages the transaction across all participating nodes.

In a distributed transaction, multiple PostgreSQL nodes may be involved in executing the transaction. When a transaction is started, the coordinator process sends a "prepare" message to each of the participating nodes, asking them to perform the transaction and prepare their commit records. Each participating node then responds to the coordinator, indicating whether it was able to successfully perform the transaction and is ready to commit.

Once all participating nodes have responded, the coordinator examines the responses and determines if all nodes are capable of committing the transaction. If so, the coordinator sends a "commit" message to each node, and the nodes then finalize their transaction and commit it to their local state.

If one or more participating nodes responds to the "prepare" message indicating that it is not able to prepare for transaction commit, the coordinator sends a "rollback" message to all participating nodes, which causes them to abort their transaction and roll back any changes made during the transaction.

2PC is vital for ensuring data consistency across multiple nodes in a distributed system. Without 2PC, it's possible for some nodes to commit the transaction while others do not, leading to inconsistent data that is difficult to reconcile. With 2PC, all nodes work in concert to ensure that the transaction is committed or rolled back as a unit.

Here is an example of how to use 2PC in a distributed transaction in Java using the 'java.sql.Connection' and 'javax.transaction.UserTransaction' classes:

```
// Create a UserTransaction object to manage the transaction
UserTransaction tx = (UserTransaction) new InitialContext().lookup("java:comp/
    UserTransaction");

// Begin the transaction
tx.begin();

// Obtain connections to each participating node
Connection node1 = DriverManager.getConnection("jdbc:postgresql://node1/
    dbname");
Connection node2 = DriverManager.getConnection("jdbc:postgresql://node2/
    dbname");

// Coordinate the distributed transaction across the nodes using 2PC
try {
    node1.setAutoCommit(false);
    node2.setAutoCommit(false);

    // Perform transactional work on each node
    // ...

    // All nodes are ready to commit, so prepare the transaction
    tx.setTransactionTimeout(60);
    tx.runTwoPhaseCommit();

    // Commit the transaction on all nodes
    node1.commit();
    node2.commit();

    // End the transaction
    tx.commit();
} catch (Exception e) {
    // Something went wrong, so roll back the transaction on all nodes
    tx.rollback();
    node1.rollback();
    node2.rollback();
} finally {
    // Close the connections
    node1.close();
    node2.close();
}
```

5.13   How do you optimize PostgreSQL's performance for geospatial data and queries using the PostGIS extension?

Optimizing PostgreSQLs performance for geospatial data and queries using the PostGIS extension requires a multi-faceted approach, which includes good database design, indexing, and query optimization. Here are some tips to help you get the most out of PostGIS:

1. Use the right spatial type: When creating tables with geospatial data, use the appropriate spatial type. PostGIS supports multiple spatial types, such as Point, LineString, Polygon, and MultiPolygon. Use the spatial type that best fits the data youre working with. Choosing the correct type can help reduce storage and improve query performance.

2. Use spatial indexes: Creating indexes on columns with geospatial data is crucial for query performance. PostGIS supports several types of indexes, such as GiST, GIN, and BRIN. Use the index thats best suited for your data and query patterns. For example, if you have data with a lot of overlapping polygons, a GIN index may be the best choice.

3. Optimize query performance: PostgreSQL includes many features for optimizing queries, such as query planning, caching, and parallel execution. Use EXPLAIN ANALYZE to analyze query performance and identify slow queries. Consider rewriting queries to take advantage of spatial indexes and other features. For example, instead of using a subquery, consider using a JOIN.

4. Use spatial functions efficiently: PostGIS includes many functions for working with geospatial data, such as ST_Distance, ST_Intersection, ST_Union, and more. Use these functions efficiently by minimizing the amount of data being processed. For example, use the ST_Intersects function to filter out non-intersecting geometries before performing a more complex operation.

Heres an example Java code that demonstrates how to create a spatial index:

```
import java.sql.*;
```

```
public class App {
    public static void main(String[] args) throws SQLException {
        String url = "jdbc:postgresql://localhost:5432/mydatabase";
        String user = "myuser";
        String password = "mypassword";

        Connection conn = DriverManager.getConnection(url, user, password);
        Statement stmt = conn.createStatement();

        String sql = "CREATE_INDEX_mytable_geom_gist_ON_mytable_USING_GIST_(
            geom);";
        stmt.executeUpdate(sql);

        stmt.close();
        conn.close();
    }
}
```

In this example, were creating a GiST index on the 'geom' column of the 'mytable' table.

Overall, optimizing PostgreSQLs performance for geospatial data and queries using PostGIS involves careful database design, efficient query patterns, and appropriate use of spatial indexes and functions. By following best practices, you can improve query response time and deliver faster, more reliable geospatial applications.

5.14   Describe the process of upgrading PostgreSQL to a newer version, including major version upgrades and the challenges involved.

Upgrading PostgreSQL to a newer version can be somewhat complicated, especially when upgrading between major versions. Here are the general steps involved in upgrading PostgreSQL:

1. Review the release notes: Before upgrading, review the release notes for the new version of PostgreSQL. It's important to understand the changes and new features in the new version, as well as any special requirements or known issues.

2. Back up your data: Before upgrading, make sure to back up all your databases and configuration files. This allows you to roll back in case something goes wrong during the upgrade process.

3. Install the new version: Install the new version of PostgreSQL using the appropriate package manager or installer for your platform. If you're upgrading between major versions, you may need to install an intermediary version first (for example, if you're upgrading from version 9.4 to version 11, you may need to first upgrade to version 9.6).

4. Migrate your data: Once the new version is installed, you'll need to migrate your data to the new version. There are different ways to do this, depending on the size of your data and the number of databases you have. One common method is to use the pg_upgrade tool, which is included with PostgreSQL. This tool allows you to upgrade an existing installation in place, without having to dump and restore your data.

5. Test and adjust: After upgrading and migrating your data, you'll need to test your applications and make any necessary adjustments. It's also a good idea to review your configuration files and make sure they're still appropriate for the new version.

Challenges involved in upgrading:

1. Compatibility issues: When upgrading between major versions, there may be compatibility issues with your applications or third-party tools that use PostgreSQL. You may need to update your applications or drivers to ensure they're compatible with the new version.

2. Configuration changes: With each new version of PostgreSQL, there are usually changes to the configuration files or options. You may need to update your configuration files to take advantage of new features, or to ensure compatibility with your specific workload.

3. Extensions and third-party modules: If you're using extensions or third-party modules with PostgreSQL, these may need to be updated or recompiled for the new version. Check with the developer or vendor of the extension or module to ensure compatibility with the new version.

Overall, upgrading PostgreSQL to a new version can be a complex process. It's important to prepare carefully and test thoroughly to ensure a successful upgrade.

5.15   What are some best practices for disaster recovery planning in a PostgreSQL environment?

Disaster recovery planning is an essential part of ensuring the continuity of a PostgreSQL environment, as unexpected downtime or data loss can cause significant business impact. The following are some best practices for disaster recovery planning in a PostgreSQL environment:

1. Regular backups: Taking regular backups is crucial for disaster recovery planning. The frequency of backups will depend on the application's criticality, but it's recommended to have at least one full backup per day. PostgreSQL offers several backup options, including pg_dump, pg_basebackup, and third-party tools like pgBackRest and Barman.

2. Test your backups: Backups are only useful if they can be restored successfully. Regularly testing backups by restoring them to a test environment is necessary to ensure backups are working correctly.

3. High availability: PostgreSQL supports several high-availability solutions such as streaming replication, logical replication, and connection pooling mechanisms like Pgpool-II and PgBouncer. These solutions can provide automatic failover and reduce downtime in the event of a disaster.

4. Monitor your system: Monitoring the PostgreSQL environment to detect any anomalies that can cause a disaster. This can involve tracking server performance, disk space, and log files. Tools like Nagios, Zabbix, and Munin can help automate the monitoring process.

5. Disaster Recovery Plan: Create a disaster recovery plan that details how the application will be restored in the event of a disaster. This plan should include steps for restoring backups, the use of high availability solutions, and a communication strategy to keep stakeholders informed.

6. Security: Ensure that your PostgreSQL environment is as secure as possible. This means using strong passwords, encrypting data in transit, encrypting backups, and implementing access controls.

7. Regular maintenance: Regular maintenance, such as vacuuming
and running analyze, can help keep PostgreSQL running smoothly
and prevent data loss. Additionally, keep PostgreSQL and its dependencies updated to avoid known vulnerabilities.

Here's an example in Java using pgBackRest for taking backups:

```
ProcessBuilder pb = new ProcessBuilder();
pb.command("pgbackrest", "backup");
Process p = pb.start();
int exitCode = p.waitFor();
if (exitCode == 0) {
    System.out.println("Backup successful");
} else {
    System.out.println("Backup failed");
}
```

In this code, pgBackRest is executed to take a backup. The exit code
is checked to see if the backup was successful or not.

5.16   Explain the role of consistency checks and validation in PostgreSQL, including tools like pg_checksums and pg_repack.

Consistency checks and validation are important for ensuring the reliability and stability of PostgreSQL databases. They help to detect
and prevent inconsistencies and errors, which can lead to data corruption or loss.

In PostgreSQL, consistency checks are performed using various mechanisms such as checksums, page verification, and transaction logs.
These mechanisms ensure that the data stored in the database is accurate and consistent.

One important tool for consistency checks in PostgreSQL is 'pg_checksums'.
This tool verifies the checksums of all pages in a database and reports
any inconsistencies. Its useful for detecting data corruption caused
by factors such as hardware failures or software bugs. Its recommended to run 'pg_checksums' regularly to detect any issues as ealy
as possible.

Another important tool is 'pg_repack'. This tool is used for data validation and optimization. It ensures that data is organized efficiently and correctly, which can improve performance. Additionally, 'pg_repack' can detect and handle data inconsistencies, which is helpful when dealing with large datasets.

In addition to these tools, its important to perform regular backups and monitor database activity to detect any abnormalities. These steps help to maintain the stability and consistency of PostgreSQL databases, and ensure that data is kept safe and secure.

Heres an example in Java for running 'pg_checksums':

```java
public static void runPgChecksums() {
    try {
        Process p = Runtime.getRuntime().exec("pg_checksums -D /var/lib/
            postgresql/data");
        p.waitFor();
        BufferedReader reader = new BufferedReader(new InputStreamReader(p.
            getInputStream()));
        String line;
        while ((line = reader.readLine()) != null) {
            System.out.println(line);
        }
    } catch (IOException e) {
        e.printStackTrace();
    } catch (InterruptedException e) {
        e.printStackTrace();
    }
}
```

This code snippet runs 'pg_checksums' on a PostgreSQL database located at '/var/lib/postgresql/data'. The output of the command is then printed to the console.

5.17 How do you integrate PostgreSQL with big data and data warehousing solutions, such as Hadoop, Apache Spark, or Amazon Redshift?

Integrating PostgreSQL with big data and data warehousing solutions can enhance the capabilities of traditional databases and provide a more scalable and efficient system for managing big data. Here are the steps to integrate PostgreSQL with some of the most popular big data and data warehousing solutions:

1. Hadoop: Hadoop is a widely used distributed processing framework
for big data. In order to integrate PostgreSQL with Hadoop, we
need to use a connector that allows PostgreSQL to read and write
data to Hadoop. One popular example is the Hadoop Connector
for PostgreSQL, which is an open-source connector that enables data
transfer between PostgreSQL and Hadoop.

Here's a Java code example that demonstrates how to use the Hadoop
Connector for PostgreSQL:

```java
import java.sql.*;

// Connect to PostgreSQL
Connection connection = DriverManager.getConnection("jdbc:postgresql://
    localhost:5432/mydatabase", "username", "password");

// Use Hadoop Connector to read data from Hadoop
Statement statement = connection.createStatement();
ResultSet result = statement.executeQuery("SELECT * FROM hdfs_table");

// Use Hadoop Connector to write data to Hadoop
PreparedStatement preparedStatement = connection.prepareStatement("INSERT
    INTO hdfs_table (column1, column2) VALUES (?, ?)");
preparedStatement.setString(1, "value1");
preparedStatement.setString(2, "value2");
preparedStatement.execute();
```

2. Apache Spark: Apache Spark is a powerful distributed computing
system that can be used for big data processing. PostgreSQL can be
integrated with Apache Spark using the JDBC driver.

Here's a Java code example that demonstrates how to use the PostgreSQL JDBC driver to read data from a PostgreSQL database into
Apache Spark:

```java
import java.sql.*;
import org.apache.spark.sql.Dataset;
import org.apache.spark.sql.Row;
import org.apache.spark.sql.SparkSession;

// Connect to PostgreSQL using the JDBC driver
Connection connection = DriverManager.getConnection("jdbc:postgresql://
    localhost:5432/mydatabase", "username", "password");

// Create a Spark session
SparkSession spark = SparkSession.builder().appName("PostgreSQLIntegration").
    master("local").getOrCreate();

// Use JDBC driver to read data from PostgreSQL
Dataset<Row> dataset = spark.read().jdbc("jdbc:postgresql://localhost:5432/
    mydatabase", "table_name", new Properties());

// Perform some transformations on the dataset
Dataset<Row> filtered = dataset.filter("column_name > 100");
```

```
// Show the results
filtered.show();
```

3. Amazon Redshift: Amazon Redshift is a cloud-based data ware-housing solution that can be used to handle large-scale data process-ing. To integrate PostgreSQL with Amazon Redshift, we need to use the Amazon Redshift JDBC driver.

Here's a Java code example that demonstrates how to use the Amazon Redshift JDBC driver to read data from Amazon Redshift into a PostgreSQL database:

```
import java.sql.*;
import com.amazon.redshift.jdbc.Driver;

// Connect to Amazon Redshift using the JDBC driver
Connection connection = DriverManager.getConnection("jdbc:redshift://redshift
    -cluster-1.cluster-cjz0oifskkiw.us-west-2.redshift.amazonaws.com:5439/
    mydatabase", "username", "password");

// Use JDBC driver to read data from Amazon Redshift
Statement statement = connection.createStatement();
ResultSet result = statement.executeQuery("SELECT␣*␣FROM␣table_name");

// Use JDBC driver to write data to PostgreSQL
Connection connection2 = DriverManager.getConnection("jdbc:postgresql://
    localhost:5432/mydatabase", "username", "password");
PreparedStatement preparedStatement = connection2.prepareStatement("INSERT␣
    INTO␣table_name␣(column1,␣column2)␣VALUES␣(?,␣?)");
while(result.next()) {
  preparedStatement.setString(1, result.getString("column1"));
  preparedStatement.setString(2, result.getString("column2"));
  preparedStatement.addBatch();
}
preparedStatement.executeBatch();
```

5.18 Discuss the challenges and techniques for optimizing PostgreSQL's performance in a cloud environment, such as AWS RDS, Google Cloud SQL, or Azure Database for PostgreSQL.

PostgreSQL is a powerful open-source relational database manage-ment system (RDBMS) that powers many applications and plat-forms. In a cloud environment, such as AWS RDS, Google Cloud

SQL, or Azure Database for PostgreSQL, there are several challenges and techniques to optimize PostgreSQL's performance.

One of the biggest challenges in a cloud environment is resource management. Cloud providers offer various configurations with different CPU, RAM, and storage options. To optimize PostgreSQL performance in such an environment, it is important to choose the right configuration based on the size of the database and expected traffic. Additionally, it's important to monitor the performance of PostgreSQL, tune the database system parameters, and leverage available cloud tools.

Here are some techniques to optimize PostgreSQL performance in a cloud environment:

1. Use managed database services: Managed database services, such as AWS RDS, Google Cloud SQL, and Azure Database for PostgreSQL, offer many benefits, such as automated backups, high availability, and system patches. By using these services, administrators can focus on performance tuning and application development, rather than database administration.

2. Optimize storage configuration: In a cloud environment, storage options can vary from magnetic disks to solid-state drives (SSDs). SSDs provide faster IO and can significantly improve PostgreSQL performance. Administrators should choose an appropriate storage configuration based on the database size and workload.

3. Leverage replication: Cloud providers offer replication options that can help improve PostgreSQL performance in a cloud environment. By replicating database instances across different zones or regions, administrators can increase availability and reduce latency for read-heavy workloads.

4. Tune system parameters: PostgreSQL has many configuration parameters that can be tuned to improve performance, such as shared_buffers, work_mem, and max_connections. In a cloud environment, the default parameters may not be optimized for the available resources. Administrators should carefully tune these parameters based on the database size, workload, and available resources. It's important to use proper benchmarks to test and validate the new configuration.

5. Use connection pooling: Connection pooling can help improve

PostgreSQL's performance by minimizing the overhead of establishing a new connection for each request. There are many connection pooling libraries available for Java, such as HikariCP and Tomcat JDBC. These libraries can be configured to optimize connection reuse and minimize lock contention.

6. Implement caching: Caching can significantly improve the performance of read-heavy workloads in PostgreSQL. Developers can leverage caching libraries, such as Memcached or Redis, to store frequently accessed data in memory. By reducing the number of read requests to the database, caching can help improve overall performance.

In conclusion, optimizing PostgreSQL's performance in a cloud environment requires careful consideration of many factors, such as resource management, system tuning, and workload characteristics. By using managed database services, optimizing storage configuration, leveraging replication, tuning system parameters, using connection pooling, and implementing caching, administrators can improve PostgreSQL performance and deliver a better user experience.

5.19   How do you manage and optimize PostgreSQL in a containerized environment using technologies like Docker and Kubernetes?

Managing and optimizing PostgreSQL in a containerized environment using technologies like Docker and Kubernetes requires a multifaceted approach. The following steps can be taken to achieve this:

1. Use an appropriate base image: A minimalistic base image that contains only the essential libraries and binaries required to run PostgreSQL can be used. This minimizes the attack surface and helps to keep the container small.

2.   Configure PostgreSQL: The PostgreSQL configuration can be tweaked to optimize its performance in a containerized environment. Some of the configuration parameters that can be tuned include shared buffers, work_mem, maintenance_work_mem, etc.

Here's an example of how to configure PostgreSQL using environment variables in a Docker container:

```
docker run -d
  -e POSTGRES_USER=myuser
  -e POSTGRES_PASSWORD=mypassword
  -e POSTGRES_DB=mydb
  -e POSTGRES_SHARED_BUFFERS=512MB
  -e POSTGRES_WORK_MEM=128MB
  -e POSTGRES_MAINTENANCE_WORK_MEM=512MB
  postgres:latest
```

In this example, the shared buffers are set to 512MB, work_mem is set to 128MB, and maintenance_work_mem is set to 512MB.

3. Persistent storage: Mounting a persistent volume to store PostgreSQL data ensures that the data is preserved even if the container is deleted. This can be achieved by using the 'volume' parameter in Docker or by using a 'PersistentVolume' in Kubernetes.

4. Resource allocation: Allocating appropriate resources to the PostgreSQL container is crucial for optimal performance. This includes CPU, memory, and disk space. In Kubernetes, this can be done through resource requests and limits.

Here's an example of how to configure resource allocation in a Kubernetes deployment:

```
apiVersion: apps/v1
kind: Deployment
metadata:
  name: postgres-deployment
spec:
  replicas: 1
  selector:
    matchLabels:
      app: postgres
  template:
    metadata:
      labels:
        app: postgres
    spec:
      containers:
      - name: postgres
        image: postgres:latest
        env:
        - name: POSTGRES_USER
          value: myuser
        - name: POSTGRES_PASSWORD
          valueFrom:
            secretKeyRef:
              name: postgres-password
              key: password
        ports:
        - containerPort: 5432
        volumeMounts:
        - mountPath: /var/lib/postgresql/data
          name: postgres-volume
        resources:
```

```
      requests:
        cpu: 500m
        memory: 512Mi
      limits:
        cpu: 1
        memory: 1Gi
  volumes:
  - name: postgres-volume
    persistentVolumeClaim:
      claimName: postgres-pvc
```

In this example, the resource requests for CPU and memory are set to 500m and 512Mi, respectively. The resource limits are set to 1 CPU and 1Gi of memory.

5. High availability: In a production environment, it's important to ensure high availability for PostgreSQL. This can be achieved by using a Master-Slave replication setup, where a primary PostgreSQL container replicates its data to one or more standby PostgreSQL containers. Kubernetes features like StatefulSets and Operators can be used to set up a High Availability PostgreSQL Cluster.

Overall, managing and optimizing PostgreSQL in a containerized environment involves considering several factors, including container configuration, resource allocation, storage, and high availability. By following best practices, you can ensure that your PostgreSQL deployment is scalable, performant, and reliable.

5.20   Describe the process of implementing advanced backup and recovery strategies in PostgreSQL, such as incremental backups, parallel backups, and synthetic backups.

Implementing advanced backup and recovery strategies in PostgreSQL involves taking advantage of several features available within the database system. The following are some of the advanced backup and recovery strategies that can be implemented in PostgreSQL:

1. Incremental Backups: PostgreSQL supports incremental backups that help reduce the backup time and the amount of data that needs

to be backed up. In incremental backups, only the changes made since the last backup are backed up, rather than the entire database. This is achieved by setting a flag called '–xid' in the 'pg_basebackup' command. It only copies WAL files that contain changes made since the last backup. A sample code block to perform an incremental backup using 'pg_basebackup' is given below:

```
pg_basebackup --checkpoint=fast --xlog --incremental --pgdata=/path/to/
       datadir --label=INCREMENTAL-BACKUP-1 /path/to/backupdir
```

2. Parallel Backups: PostgreSQL provides the ability to perform parallel backups to take advantage of multi-core CPUs. This feature helps to reduce the backup time and speed up the recovery time in case of a disaster. Parallel backups can be performed using the pg_dump utility, which divides the backup into multiple parts that can be run simultaneously. Code snippet to illustrate performing parallel backups using pg_dump is shown below:

```
pg_dump -Fd -j 4 -f /path/to/backupdir dbname
```

Here, '-j' option specifies the number of parallel processes, and '-Fd' specifies the output format.

3. Synthetic Backups: A synthetic backup is a full backup that is created by merging an initial full backup with subsequent incremental backups. Synthetic backups help reduce the recovery time by providing a single backup that contains all the changes since the last full backup. Synthetic backups can be created using tools like pgBackRest and Barman. An example code snippet to illustrate performing synthetic backups using pgBackRest is shown below:

```
pgbackrest --stanza=db backup --type=synthetic
```

The above command creates a synthetic backup of the 'db' cluster using pgBackRest.

In summary, implementing advanced backup and recovery strategies in PostgreSQL requires taking advantage of features such as incremental backups, parallel backups, and synthetic backups. The use of the appropriate backup strategy depends on the backup size, business needs and the database environment infrastructure.

Chapter 6

Guru

6.1 Discuss the process of contributing to the PostgreSQL open-source project, including the PostgreSQL community, mailing lists, and the patch submission and review process.

Contributing to an open-source project like PostgreSQL requires a good understanding of the community, mailing lists, and the patch submission and review process.

PostgreSQL community: The PostgreSQL community is a vibrant community of developers, users, and contributors who are passionate about this open-source RDBMS. The community thrives on active participation and contribution, including code contributions, documentation, testing, and technical discussions.

Mailing Lists: The PostgreSQL community uses several mailing lists to communicate and collaborate. These lists serve as forums for discussions related to development, user support, documentation, and testing. The most important mailing lists are-

- Pgsql-hackers: This list is specifically for developers and contributors to discuss the development of PostgreSQL.

- Pgsql-general: This list is for general user questions and support.

- Pgsql-docs: This list is for documentation discussions and contributions.

Patch submission and review process: Before submitting a patch, it's important to follow certain guidelines and best practices to ensure it's of high quality, well-documented, and compatible with the PostgreSQL codebase. Here are the general steps involved in submitting a patch:

1. Fork the PostgreSQL repository and create a branch for your changes.

2. Make your changes or additions and document them as thoroughly as possible.

3. Ensure that you run the tests to confirm that your changes did not break any code.

4. Create a patch file which contains your changes.

5. Submit the patch to the pgsql-hackers mailing list for review.

Reviewing patch process: The PostgreSQL community values code quality and ensuring that submitted patches are reviewed thoroughly. The following steps outline the process of reviewing patch submissions:

1. Other experienced contributors in the community will review the patch and provide feedback.

2. They may suggest changes or make observations that may need to be addressed.

3. After the issues are resolved, the patch is ready to be committed to the PostgreSQL codebase.

Overall, contributing to the PostgreSQL open-source project is an exciting and rewarding experience for anyone interested in becoming a part of the software engineering community.

6.2 Explain how PostgreSQL's query planner utilizes statistics and histograms for query optimization and how to influence its behavior.

In PostgreSQL, the query planner utilizes statistics and histograms to estimate the number of rows that will be returned by a given query, in order to optimize the plan for execution. The statistics and histograms are based on data collected by the PostgreSQL planner over time, with the goal of allowing it to make accurate estimates about how many rows a given query will return.

Statistics are collected on columns and indexes, including information such as the number of distinct values in a column, the minimum and maximum values, the most common values, and the distribution of values across the column. Histograms are a more detailed form of statistics, which divide the range of values in a column into buckets and record the number of rows that fall within each bucket.

For example, suppose we have a table of users, with columns for name, age, and gender. If we want to find the average age of all male users, the planner can use the statistics on the gender column to estimate how many rows will be returned for male users, and then use the histogram on the age column to estimate the average age of those users.

Influence on behavior: PostgreSQL provides a few ways to influence the behavior of the query planner with regards to statistics and histograms.

1. The ANALYZE command can be used to collect fresh statistics and histograms on a table or index.

2. The auto_explain module can be used to log the plans of slow or expensive queries, allowing us to examine how the planner is making use of statistics and histograms.

3. The statistics_target setting can be used to increase or decrease the level of detail in the statistics and histograms collected by the planner.

To conclude, statistics and histograms are a critical component of the PostgreSQL query planner, allowing it to make accurate estimates of the number of rows a query will return and optimizing the plan for execution. Developers can influence the behavior of the planner through various settings to ensure it uses the right data in the right way to optimize query execution.

6.3 Describe the internals of PostgreSQL's indexing mechanisms, including B-trees, GiST, SP-GiST, GIN, and RUM indexes, and their use cases.

PostgreSQL supports a wide range of indexing mechanisms to provide efficient and optimized access paths to the data stored in tables. Following are the different types of indexing mechanisms supported by PostgreSQL:

1. B-tree Indexes: B-tree indexes are the default indexing mechanism used by PostgreSQL. It is a balanced tree structure that stores all the values in sorted order, allowing for efficient range queries, searching, and sorting operations. B-tree indexes work best when the indexed column has low cardinality, i.e., values are frequently repeated.

Example: Lets say, we have a table named employees with columns id, name, and salary. To create a B-tree index on salary column, we can use the below SQL query.

```
CREATE INDEX employees_salary_idx ON employees (salary);
```

2. GiST Indexes: GiST stands for Generalized Search Tree. It is an advanced indexing mechanism that can work with a variety of data types such as geometric and full-text data. It uses custom operators implemented by the user to perform the index operations. GiST can be used for spatial indexing as well.

Example: Lets say we have a table named books with columns id, title, author, and genre. To create a GiST index on title column, we can use the below SQL query.

```
CREATE INDEX books_title_idx ON books USING gist (title gist_trgm_ops);
```

3. SP-GiST Indexes: SP-GiST stands for Space-Partitioned Generalized Search Tree. It is similar to GiST, but it is more space-efficient as it partitions the index into smaller sub-trees. SP-GiST is best suited when the data is highly skewed or imbalanced.

Example: Lets say, we have a table named products with columns id, name, brand, and category. To create an SP-GIST index on brand column, we can use the below SQL query.

```
CREATE INDEX products_brand_idx ON products USING spgist (brand);
```

4. GIN Indexes: GIN stands for Generalized Inverted Index. It is best suited for indexing arrays and other composite data types. GIN creates an index entry for each element in the array, which allows it to quickly match all rows that contain the specified element(s).

Example: Lets say, we have a table named posts with the column tags which stores an array of tags associated with each post. To create a GIN index on tags column, we can use the following SQL query.

```
CREATE INDEX posts_tags_gin_idx ON posts USING gin (tags);
```

5. RUM Indexes: RUM stands for Row-Used Memory. It is similar to GIN but is specifically designed to handle distinct values. RUM indexes allow indexing of operations like similarity queries and text-search-based queries.

Example: Lets say we have a table named customers with the column address which stores textual location data. To create a RUM index on address column, we can use the following SQL query.

```
CREATE INDEX customers_address_rum_idx ON customers USING rum (address
    rum_ops);
```

Each of these indexing mechanisms is designed to handle specific use cases efficiently. B-tree indexes are the most commonly used indexing mechanism, but PostgreSQL provides many advanced indexing mechanisms geared toward specific types of data and indexing requirements.

6.4   How do you diagnose and resolve performance bottlenecks in PostgreSQL using advanced profiling and diagnostic tools, such as perf, gdb, and DTrace?

Diagnosing and resolving performance bottlenecks in PostgreSQL using advanced profiling and diagnostic tools require a deep understanding of both PostgreSQL and the tools themselves. Here are the steps to accomplish this:

Step 1: Identify the performance bottleneck The first step in diagnosing and resolving performance bottlenecks is to identify the bottleneck. There are many possible bottlenecks, including CPU-bound queries, I/O-bound queries, contention for shared resources, etc. One way to do this is to use PostgreSQL's built-in query profiling tools, such as 'EXPLAIN' and 'EXPLAIN ANALYZE', to analyze the execution plan of a query.

Another way is to use external profiling tools like 'perf', 'gdb', and 'DTrace'. These tools enable you to monitor system-level performance metrics such as CPU usage, disk I/O, network activity, and more.

Step 2: Collect Performance Data Once you have identified a potential bottleneck, you need to collect performance data to understand exactly what is happening in the system. Here are some suggested tools and techniques to use:

- PostgreSQL's built-in statistics collector provides detailed information about query execution time, index usage, and more.

- 'perf' is a powerful Linux profiling tool that can be used to measure various system-level performance metrics such as CPU utilization, cache hits and misses, and memory usage.

- 'gdb' is a command-line tool that can be used to debug and analyze the behavior of a running process. It can be used to examine the state of the PostgreSQL process, set breakpoints, and analyze the execution of specific queries.

- 'DTrace' is a dynamic tracing tool that can be used to monitor and profile system-level activities on FreeBSD, NetBSD, macOS, and other Unix-based systems. It allows you to create custom tracing scripts that can be used to examine the behavior of the PostgreSQL process and identify performance issues.

Step 3: Analyze Performance Data Next, you need to analyze the performance data that you've collected. Depending on the tool used, this might involve examining system-level performance metrics, query execution plans, or source code-level information. From this analysis, you should be able to identify specific areas that are causing performance issues, such as inefficient queries or resource contention.

Step 4: Resolve Performance Issues After identifying and analyzing the performance bottleneck, you can take steps to resolve it. Depending on the specific issue, this might involve optimizing queries or database schema, tuning server parameters, or upgrading hardware resources.

In conclusion, diagnosing and resolving performance bottlenecks in PostgreSQL requires a deep understanding of PostgreSQL and the associated diagnostic tools. By following the steps outlined above, you can identify and resolve performance bottlenecks and improve the overall performance of your PostgreSQL system.

6.5 Discuss the process of benchmarking and stress-testing PostgreSQL deployments using tools like pgbench, sysbench, and TPC-C/TPC-H benchmarks.

Benchmarking and stress-testing are essential for determining the capacity and the limits of a PostgreSQL deployment. These tasks involve simulating the behavior of a database under different loads and conditions and measuring its performance and stability. In this answer, I will discuss the main tools and techniques used for benchmarking and stress-testing PostgreSQL deployments, with a focus on pgbench, sysbench, and TPC-C/TPC-H benchmarks.

Benchmarking with pgbench

Pgbench is a simple tool that comes bundled with PostgreSQL and allows you to simulate an OLTP workload on a PostgreSQL database. With pgbench, you can define a workload consisting of a set of SQL statements that represent typical transactions in your application. You can configure the number of clients that will perform the workload concurrently and the duration of the test.

Pgbench generates a synthetic workload based on the specified parameters and measures the transaction rate and the response time of the database. The results can be analyzed to determine the maximum sustainable transaction rate (TPS) and the latency of the database under various loads.

Here's an example of how to use pgbench to benchmark a PostgreSQL database:

```
import java.sql.*;

public class PgBenchTest {
  public static void main(String[] args) {
    try {
      Class.forName("org.postgresql.Driver");
      Connection conn = DriverManager.getConnection("jdbc:postgresql://
          localhost/mydb", "myuser", "mypassword");
      Statement stmt = conn.createStatement();
      ResultSet rs = stmt.executeQuery("SELECT pgbench_accounts;");
      while (rs.next()) {
        int accounts = rs.getInt(1);
        System.out.println("pgbench_accounts = " + accounts);
      }
      stmt.close();
      conn.close();
    } catch (Exception e) {
      e.printStackTrace();
    }
  }
}
```

This code connects to a PostgreSQL database, retrieves the current value of the 'pgbench_accounts' configuration parameter (which specifies the number of accounts in the pgbench schema), and prints it to the console.

To run the benchmark, you can use the following command:

```
pgbench -c 10 -j 2 -t 1000 -U myuser -p 5432 -d mydb
```

This command runs pgbench with 10 clients (-c), each running two threads (-j) and executing 1000 transactions (-t) against the database named "mydb" on port 5432, using the user "myuser". The results are printed to the console.

Stress-testing with sysbench

Sysbench is a more powerful tool for benchmarking and stress-testing PostgreSQL deployments. It can simulate a wide range of workloads, including OLTP, read-only, and write-only scenarios, as well as more complex workloads involving joins and subqueries. Sysbench can also generate random data, which can be useful for testing performance under realistic conditions.

To use sysbench with PostgreSQL, you need to install the PostgreSQL driver plugin:

```
sudo apt-get install postgresql-server-dev-XX
cd sysbench
./configure --with-pgsql
make
sudo make install
```

After installing sysbench, you can create a test database and run the benchmark using the following commands:

```
createdb sbtest
pgbench -i -s 100 sbtest
sysbench --test=oltp --db-driver=pgsql --oltp-table-size=1000000 --num-
    threads=8 --max-time=60 --max-requests=0 --pgsql-db=sbtest --pgsql-user=
    myuser --pgsql-password=mypassword --pgsql-port=5432 --oltp-read-only=on
    run
```

This command creates a database named "sbtest" and initializes it with pgbench data scaled to a factor of 100 (-s 100). The sysbench command then runs an OLTP workload with one million rows in the main table (-oltp-table-size), eight threads (-num-threads), and a runtime of 60 seconds (-max-time) with unlimited requests (-max-requests). The database connection details and credentials are specified with the –pgsql-* options.

The TPC benchmarks

The Transaction Processing Council (TPC) is an independent organization that develops benchmarks for measuring the performance of database systems. The most well-known TPC benchmarks for PostgreSQL are TPC-C and TPC-H.

TPC-C simulates an OLTP workload consisting of a set of transactions that involve inserting, updating, deleting, and querying records in a database. The workload is designed to represent a typical online transaction processing system.

TPC-H simulates a decision support system workload consisting of complex queries over large datasets. The queries involve aggregation, join, and filtering operations typical of data warehousing and business intelligence applications.

To run a TPC benchmark, you need to obtain the benchmark kit from the TPC website and follow the instructions provided. Running a TPC benchmark requires significant resources, including a large amount of memory, storage, and processing power. Therefore, it is mainly used by vendors and organizations that need to evaluate the performance of database systems for their specific workloads.

In conclusion, benchmarking and stress-testing PostgreSQL deployments are essential for ensuring the performance and scalability of database systems. The tools and techniques discussed in this answer, including pgbench, sysbench, and TPC benchmarks, provide different levels of complexity and sophistication for simulating various workloads and measuring performance metrics. When using these tools, it is essential to design realistic and representative workloads and to interpret the results carefully to draw meaningful conclusions about database performance.

6.6   Explain the internals of PostgreSQL's concurrency control mechanisms, including lock management, deadlocks, and lock escalation.

PostgreSQL implements a multiversion concurrency control (MVCC) mechanism to provide high concurrency while maintaining data consistency. MVCC allows multiple transactions to access the same data simultaneously while preventing them from interfering with each other. To achieve this, PostgreSQL uses locks to provide serializability and isolation between transactions.

Lock Management

PostgreSQL provides two types of locks: shared locks and exclusive locks. Shared locks allow multiple transactions to read the same data simultaneously, while exclusive locks prevent other transactions from reading or writing the same data. Transactions acquire and release locks explicitly by requesting a lock on a particular table or row.

PostgreSQL uses a lock table to manage locks. Whenever a transaction requests a lock, PostgreSQL checks the lock table to see if the requested lock conflicts with any existing locks. If there is no conflict, the transaction is granted the lock and the lock table is updated. If there is a conflict, the transaction is blocked until the conflicting lock is released.

Deadlocks

A deadlock occurs when two or more transactions are waiting for each other to release the locks they hold. Deadlocks can cause transactions to hang indefinitely, which can lead to a serious performance problem. PostgreSQL detects deadlocks by maintaining a wait-for graph. Whenever a transaction requests a lock that conflicts with an existing lock, a directed edge is added to the wait-for graph. If the wait-for graph contains a cycle, a deadlock has occurred. PostgreSQL resolves deadlocks by rolling back one of the transactions involved in the deadlock.

Lock Escalation

Lock escalation is the process of converting multiple low-level locks into fewer higher-level locks to reduce lock contention and improve performance. In PostgreSQL, lock escalation is not automatic and is not performed by the database itself. Lock escalation must be explicitly requested by the application. For example, an application might request a table-level lock instead of requesting individual row-level locks for a large number of rows. Lock escalation can be a useful optimization in certain situations, but it can also increase the risk of deadlocks.

In conclusion, PostgreSQL provides a robust concurrency control mechanism using locks, and it also provides advanced features like MVCC, wait-for graphs, and deadlock detection to ensure data consistency and prevent performance problems caused by concurrency.

Application developers need to be careful with lock management to ensure that they don't introduce performance problems or deadlocks.

6.7   Describe the architecture of PostgreSQL's streaming replication and how it can be extended or customized for specific use cases.

PostgreSQL's streaming replication is a feature that allows continuous, mirrored replication of a live database to one or more standby servers. The architecture of PostgreSQL's streaming replication consists of two main components: the primary server and the standby servers.

The primary server is the live database server that accepts client connections and processes write transactions. The primary server continuously streams its write-ahead logs (WALs) to the standby servers where they are applied to the standby's database. The WALs are a sequence of log records that contain the changes made to the database by each transaction.

The standby servers are replicas of the primary server that continuously receive and apply the WALs to their own database. They are in a "hot standby" mode, meaning they can accept read-only queries from clients. If the primary server fails, one of the standby servers can be promoted to become the new primary server and continue serving clients. This feature provides a robust and fault-tolerant solution for high availability.

PostgreSQL's streaming replication can be extended and customized for specific use cases using the following methods:

1. Logical Replication: This feature allows individual tables or subsets of a database to be replicated to other databases. Logical replication is preferable when fine-grained control is required for replicating certain subsets of data. It involves the use of replication slots and a replication protocol to move data between servers.

2. Batch Streaming Replication: Introduces a batch mode that enables batched streaming of WALs between master and standby servers. In this mode, the replication stream is split into packets and can be more efficiently transferred over slow or unreliable networks.

3. Multi-master Replication: PostgreSQL also supports multi-master replication where two or more nodes coordinate to accept read/write transactions, and each node replicates changes made by the other nodes. Multi-master replication allows for distributed systems where there is no single node that needs to be trusted with updates.

4. Replication Slots: PostgreSQL's replication slots provide a way to maintain a consistent state for standby servers by keeping track of the WALs that have already been processed. Replication slots ensure that old WALs are not recycled, ensuring that standby servers will be able to catch up to the primary server when they have been disconnected.

5. Custom Recovery: PostgreSQL's recovery process can be customized in several ways such as specifying which WAL files to restore from the archive, running additional scripts before and after recovery, and changing the settings for the new primary server. Custom recovery allows different types of recovery scenarios to be implemented and customized according to specific requirements.

Here's an example of how to set up a streaming replication in Java, using the PostgreSQL JDBC driver:

```java
public class ReplicationSetup {
  public static void main(String[] args) {
    String primaryUrl = "jdbc:postgresql://primary-server/db";
    String standbyUrl = "jdbc:postgresql://standby-server/db";
    Properties props = new Properties();
    props.setProperty("user", "username");
    props.setProperty("password", "password");

    try(Connection primaryConn = DriverManager.getConnection(primaryUrl, props
        );
      Statement primaryStmt = primaryConn.createStatement();) {
      // enable WAL archiving on primary server
      primaryStmt.execute("ALTER SYSTEM SET wal_level = replica");
      primaryStmt.execute("ALTER SYSTEM SET archive_mode = on");
      primaryStmt.execute("ALTER SYSTEM SET archive_command = 'rsync %p /
          pgdata/wal_archive/%f'");
      primaryStmt.execute("SELECT pg_reload_conf()");

      // create a replication user on primary server
      primaryStmt.execute("CREATE USER replication WITH REPLICATION PASSWORD '
          password'");

      // create a replication slot on primary server
      primaryStmt.execute("SELECT * FROM pg_create_physical_replication_slot('
          standby_slot')");
```

```
// create a replication configuration file on standby server
String configFile = "/pgdata/postgresql.conf";
Files.write(Paths.get(configFile), Arrays.asList(
  "primary_conninfo␣=␣'host=primary-server␣user=replication␣password=
       password'",
  "standby_mode␣=␣'on'",
  "primary_slot_name␣=␣'standby_slot'"
));

// start the standby server
ProcessBuilder pb = new ProcessBuilder("pg_ctl", "-D", "/pgdata", "start
    ");
pb.redirectErrorStream(true);
pb.redirectOutput(ProcessBuilder.Redirect.INHERIT);
pb.start();
} catch (SQLException | IOException ex) {
ex.printStackTrace();
}
}
}
```

In this example, we set up WAL archiving on the primary server,
create a replication user and slot, and create a configuration file on
the standby server. Finally, we start the standby server, which will
start replicating changes from the primary server. This is just a basic
example; in practice, additional configuration and monitoring steps
would be required to ensure robust and efficient replication.

6.8   Discuss the process of designing and implementing custom PostgreSQL extensions, including new data types, operators, and functions.

PostgreSQL, being an open-source relational database management
system (RDBMS), allows developers to extend its functionality by
designing and implementing custom extensions. With custom extensions, developers can add new data types, operators, and functions
according to their application requirements. The following is a detailed process of designing and implementing custom PostgreSQL extensions:

1. Design the Extension

The first step is to design the extension by identifying the requirements that it should meet. This step involves understanding the data types, operators, and functions that the extension will need to support. Ideally, the extension should align with the principles of SQL, such as typesafety, nullability, and immutability.

2. Choose Extension Type

There are three types of PostgreSQL extensions: C-language extensions, SQL-language extensions, and procedural language extensions. The type of extension you choose determines the language and tools you use to create it.

C-language extensions are implemented purely in C programming language and are used to add new data types and operators.

SQL-language extensions are implemented in SQL and used to create new functions, which utilize existing data types and operators.

Procedural language extensions allow you to extend PostgreSQL with new programming languages like Python or Perl.

3. Create the Extension

Once you have decided on the extension type, the next step is to create the extension.

For C-language extensions, developers write the necessary C code to implement the new data types, operators, or functions.

For SQL-language extensions, developers typically create new functions using PostgreSQL's procedural language PL/pgSQL.

For procedural language extensions, developers need to install the procedures for the specific scripting or programming language.

4. Build and Install the Extension

After creating the extension, it needs to be built and installed. With C-language extensions, developers will need to create a makefile with instructions to compile the extension. Developers can use PostgreSQL's build infrastructure to handle this process automatically.

For SQL-language extensions, developers only need to run a SQL script that creates the necessary functions, but may also need to grant permissions to appropriate roles.

5. Test and Deploy the Extension

Finally, the extension needs to be tested thoroughly to ensure that it is working correctly. Testing should include unit tests for data types, operators, and functions created by the extension. Once testing is complete, the extension is ready for deployment.

In summary, designing and implementing custom PostgreSQL extensions involves designing the extension, choosing the extension type, creating the extension, building and installing the extension and finally testing and deploying it. While developing extensions, it is recommended to follow PostgreSQL best practices, write clean and efficient code, and use user-friendly interfaces to ensure the extension is easy to use by others.

6.9   How do you integrate PostgreSQL with machine learning and AI solutions, such as TensorFlow, PyTorch, or scikit-learn, for advanced data analysis?

Integrating PostgreSQL with machine learning libraries such as TensorFlow, PyTorch, and scikit-learn can be achieved in several ways. Here are some of the most popular methods:

1. Use SQL to extract data to CSV or other formats, and then load the data into the machine learning library. This method involves writing SQL queries to extract data from PostgreSQL tables, exporting the data to CSV files, and then loading the CSV files into a machine learning library. For example, this can be done in Java with the following code:

```
import java.sql.*;
import java.io.*;
import com.opencsv.*;

public class PostgreSqlToCsv {
  public static void main(String[] args) throws SQLException {
    String url = "jdbc:postgresql://localhost/testdb";
```

```
    String user = "testuser";
    String password = "password";
    Connection conn = DriverManager.getConnection(url, user, password);

    String sql = "SELECT * FROM mytable";
    Statement stmt = conn.createStatement();
    ResultSet rs = stmt.executeQuery(sql);

    CSVWriter writer = new CSVWriter(new FileWriter("data.csv"));
    while (rs.next()) {
      String[] record = new String[2];
      record[0] = rs.getString("column1");
      record[1] = rs.getString("column2");
      writer.writeNext(record);
    }
    writer.close();
  }
}
```

2. Use a JDBC driver to execute SQL queries from within the machine
learning library. This method allows you to execute SQL queries
directly from within your machine learning code, without the need
to export data to CSV files. For example, in Java, you can use the
PostgreSQL JDBC driver to execute SQL queries like this:

```
import java.sql.*;

public class PostgreSqlQuery {
  public static void main(String[] args) throws SQLException {
    String url = "jdbc:postgresql://localhost/testdb";
    String user = "testuser";
    String password = "password";
    Connection conn = DriverManager.getConnection(url, user, password);

    String sql = "SELECT * FROM mytable";
    Statement stmt = conn.createStatement();
    ResultSet rs = stmt.executeQuery(sql);

    while (rs.next()) {
      String column1 = rs.getString("column1");
      String column2 = rs.getString("column2");
      // do something with the data...
    }
  }
}
```

3. Use a third-party library or framework that provides integration
with PostgreSQL. There are several open-source and commercial libraries and frameworks that provide integration with PostgreSQL
and machine learning libraries. For example, Apache Spark provides
a DataFrame API that can be used to read data from PostgreSQL
and perform machine learning tasks. Here's an example of how to
load a PostgreSQL table into a Spark DataFrame in Java:

```
import org.apache.spark.sql.*;

public class PostgreSqlToDataFrame {
```

```
    public static void main(String[] args) {
      SparkSession spark = SparkSession.builder()
            .appName("PostgreSQL␣to␣DataFrame")
            .master("local[*]")
            .getOrCreate();

      Dataset<Row> df = spark.read()
            .format("jdbc")
            .option("url", "jdbc:postgresql://localhost/testdb")
            .option("dbtable", "mytable")
            .option("user", "testuser")
            .option("password", "password")
            .load();

      df.show();
    }
  }
```

Once you have loaded the data from PostgreSQL into your machine
learning library, you can use the library's APIs to perform various
machine learning tasks, such as training and evaluating models, making predictions, and visualizing results. The specific API you use will
depend on the library you are using and the task you are performing.
Consult the library's documentation for more details.

6.10   Explain the role of query parallelism in PostgreSQL and how it can be fine-tuned for different workloads and hardware configurations.

PostgreSQL supports query parallelism which enables it to execute
queries using multiple CPU cores simultaneously. This feature im-
proves the overall throughput of a query workload by distributing the
workload among multiple CPUs.

By default, PostgreSQL uses a parallel query executor for larger table
scans and joins, but it can be configured to use parallelism for other
query types such as index scans and sorts. The degree of parallelism
is determined dynamically by the system and can be controlled by
modifying configuration parameters such as 'max_worker_processes',
'max_parallel_workers_per_gather', and
'max_parallel_maintenance_workers'.

To fine-tune PostgreSQL for different workloads and hardware configurations, administrators should consider the following factors:

1. Table partitioning - dividing large tables into smaller partitions can improve parallelism since each partition can be scanned simultaneously.

2. Workload characterization - identifying the types of queries being run and their resource requirements can help determine the ideal degree of parallelism. For example, some query types may benefit from higher degree of parallelism than others.

3. System hardware - the number of CPU cores, memory capacity and I/O bandwidth of the system determine the maximum degree of parallelism that can be achieved. Allocating appropriate resources to the PostgreSQL instance can improve parallelism and overall performance.

To illustrate this concept in Java, consider the following code segment that simulates parallel query execution using a simple partitioning scheme:

```
ExecutorService executor = Executors.newFixedThreadPool(numThreads);
List<Future<Integer>> results = new ArrayList<>();

for (int i = 0; i < numPartitions; i++) {
    final int partition = i;
    Future<Integer> result = executor.submit(() -> {
        int sum = 0;
        try (PreparedStatement stmt = conn.prepareStatement(
                "SELECT␣SUM(column)␣FROM␣table␣WHERE␣partition␣=␣?")) {
            stmt.setInt(1, partition);
            ResultSet rs = stmt.executeQuery();
            if (rs.next()) {
                sum = rs.getInt(1);
            }
        }
        return sum;
    });
    results.add(result);
}

int total = 0;
for (Future<Integer> result : results) {
    total += result.get();
}
```

In this example, we are executing a parallel query by dividing a large table into smaller partitions, and then submitting each partition to a separate worker thread for execution. The results from each partition are then combined to obtain the final query result.

This approach can be extended to support more sophisticated partitioning schemes and query types, depending on the specific workload characteristics and hardware configuration.

6.11 Describe the internals of PostgreSQL's transaction log, including log truncation, log shipping, and checkpointing.

PostgreSQL's transaction log is also known as the WAL (Write-Ahead Logging) system. It is responsible for ensuring data durability, high availability, and crash recovery. The WAL system relies on a sequential log of all changes made to the database, which can be used to recreate the database state in case of a crash or a failure.

The WAL system works by persistently writing all changes to the database to the log before applying them to the actual database. This ensures that even in the event of a crash or a system failure, the data changes are still intact and can be recovered.

The WAL system has three main components:

1. WAL buffer
2. WAL segments
3. Checkpoints

1. WAL buffer: The WAL buffer is a memory buffer used to store the latest changes to the database. When a transaction is committed, its changes are first written to the WAL buffer, and then to the WAL segments. The WAL buffer has a fixed size, and it is flushed to disk when it becomes full, or when a checkpoint occurs.

2. WAL segments: The WAL segments are individual files that make up the complete WAL. Each segment has a fixed size (usually 16 MB) and is written sequentially. Once a segment is filled, the WAL writer switches to a new segment file. The WAL segment files can be archived and shipped to other servers for replication and disaster recovery purposes.

3. Checkpoints: Checkpoints are a mechanism to ensure data consistency and limit the recovery time in the case of a crash or failure. The checkpoint process writes a special record to the WAL, indicating that all changes up to that point have been fully written to disk. This record also contains metadata that helps to speed up the crash recovery process. Additionally, checkpoints allow for the WAL segments to be safely truncated, ensuring that the disk space used by the WAL does not grow uncontrollably.

Log shipping is one way to replicate the WAL to another server. This ensures that the WAL is available to another server if the primary server fails or goes offline. Log shipping works by copying the WAL segments from the primary server to the standby server. The standby server applies the changes in the WAL segments, and it can take over as the primary server in case of a failure. PostgreSQL's pg_receivexlog utility is used to receive and write the WAL data received from the primary server.

Truncating the WAL is the process of removing older WAL segments, which are no longer needed for recovery purposes. The WAL segments can be truncated once all changes up to the checkpoint before those segments have been persisted to disk on all replication targets. Once the WAL segments have been safely replicated, they can be safely removed from the primary server to make space for newly created WAL segments. The 'pg_archivecleanup' utility can be used to purge archived WAL segments from a pg_xlog directory while preserving keep these files that are necessary for use with streaming replication.

In summary, PostgreSQL's WAL system ensures the durability of all database changes by writing them to a sequential log. The WAL segments can be archived and shipped to other servers for replication and disaster recovery purposes, while checkpoints ensure that the WAL segments can be safely truncated, and WAL data are available for recovery purposes if needed.

6.12 Discuss the challenges and solutions for PostgreSQL deployments in hybrid or multi-cloud environments, including data synchronization and latency concerns.

PostgreSQL deployments in hybrid or multi-cloud environments can present unique challenges compared to more traditional database deployments due to factors such as data synchronization, latency, and network connectivity. However, there are solutions available to help overcome these challenges.

One of the biggest challenges for PostgreSQL deployments in hybrid or multi-cloud environments is data synchronization, particularly when multiple instances of the database are running across multiple cloud providers or on-premise data centers. Ensuring consistency across all instances of the database can be difficult, especially when different providers offer different replication options.

One solution is to use a database replication technology that can operate across multiple cloud providers, such as logical replication or Bucardo, which can replicate data from one PostgreSQL instance to another without relying on the physical structure of the servers involved. This can enable cross-provider replication and help ensure consistency across all instances of the database.

Latency concerns are also a significant challenge for PostgreSQL deployments in hybrid or multi-cloud environments, particularly when data needs to be accessed quickly from different locations. Network delays can significantly impact performance, leading to slow query response times and other issues.

One solution is to deploy the database closer to the applications that access it. Cloud providers typically have multiple availability zones across different geographical regions, and deploying the database in a zone closer to the application can help reduce latency concerns.

Another solution is to use connection pooling technologies, such as PgBouncer, which can help reduce the number of connections needed between the application and database. This can help reduce network delays and speed up data retrieval.

Lastly, it's important to ensure the network connectivity between instances of the database in different cloud providers or data centers is robust and reliable. This can involve using high-speed networking and investing in security measures to ensure data privacy and prevent unauthorized access.

In summary, PostgreSQL deployments in hybrid or multi-cloud environments often require specific solutions to overcome challenges related to data synchronization, latency, and network connectivity. By using replication technologies that can operate across multiple providers, deploying the database closer to applications, using connection pooling, and ensuring network connectivity is robust and secure, it's possible to create a reliable and high-performing database deployment in hybrid or multi-cloud environments.

6.13 How do you design and implement advanced sharding and partitioning schemes in PostgreSQL to handle massive amounts of data and complex workloads?

PostgreSQL offers a number of features to support sharding and partitioning to help you manage and scale your database as your data grows. Here is an overview of how you can design and implement advanced sharding and partitioning schemes in PostgreSQL to handle massive amounts of data and complex workloads:

1. Determine Your Sharding Strategy: Sharding is the process of distributing data across multiple nodes in a database cluster. There are several sharding strategies available, including range, hash, and list sharding. Range sharding distributes data based on a specific range of values in a column, while hash sharding distributes data based on a hash function applied to a column. List sharding distributes data based on a specified list of values in a column. You need to analyze your data and workload patterns to determine which sharding strategy would be the best fit for your use case.

2. Choose Your Partitioning Strategy: Partitioning is the process of dividing a large table into smaller, more manageable partitions. Partitioning can improve query performance by reducing the amount of data that needs to be scanned. There are several partitioning strategies available in PostgreSQL, including range, hash, and list partitioning. Range partitioning divides a table based on a specified range of values in a partitioning column, while hash partitioning divides a table based on a hash function applied to a partitioning column. List partitioning divides a table based on a specified list of values in a partitioning column. You need to consider your data access patterns and query patterns to determine which partitioning strategy would be the most appropriate for your use case.

3. Implement Your Sharding and Partitioning Scheme: Once you have determined your sharding and partitioning strategy, the next step is to create the appropriate tables, indexes, and constraints to implement your scheme. For example, to implement range partitioning, you need to specify the partitioning column and the partition bounds for each partition. You can then create indexes on the partitioning column to improve query performance.

4. Choose an appropriate Connection Pooling Mechanism: Connection pooling is a technique that allows you to reuse database connections instead of creating a new connection for each transaction. Connection pooling is important for sharded and partitioned databases because it helps to reduce the overhead of establishing new connections to each node. There are several connection pooling mechanisms available, including PgBouncer, Pgpool-II, and JDBC connection pooling.

5. Monitor and Tune Your Sharded and Partitioned Database: Finally, it is important to monitor and tune your sharded and partitioned database to ensure that it is performing optimally. You should monitor database metrics such as CPU usage, memory usage, I/O operations, and query performance to identify any performance bottlenecks. You can use tools like PostgreSQL's pg_stat_activity view, and pg_stat_database and pg_stat_user tables to monitor database activity. You should also perform tuning tasks like index optimization, query optimization, and configuration tuning to ensure that your database is performing optimally.

Here is an example of how you can implement a range partitioning scheme in PostgreSQL using Java:

```
public void createPartitionedTable() {
    Connection conn = dataSource.getConnection();
    try {
        Statement stmt = conn.createStatement();
        String sql = "CREATE TABLE my_table (id INTEGER, value TEXT) PARTITION
            BY RANGE (id)";
        stmt.executeUpdate(sql);

        sql = "CREATE TABLE my_table_p0 PARTITION OF my_table FOR VALUES FROM
            (0) TO (100)";
        stmt.executeUpdate(sql);

        sql = "CREATE TABLE my_table_p1 PARTITION OF my_table FOR VALUES FROM
            (100) TO (200)";
        stmt.executeUpdate(sql);

        sql = "CREATE INDEX my_table_id_idx ON my_table (id)";
        stmt.executeUpdate(sql);
    }
    finally {
        conn.close();
    }
}
```

This code creates a new table called "my_table" and partitions it based on the "id" column using range partitioning. It creates two partitions, "my_table_p0" and "my_table_p1", with partition bounds defined as (0, 100) and (100, 200), respectively. It also creates an index on the "id" column to improve query performance.

Remember that sharding and partitioning can be complex, and it is critical to consider your use case carefully before implementing a sharding and partitioning scheme. You should also test your scheme extensively to ensure that it performs well under high load and stress conditions.

6.14 Explain the internals of PostgreSQL's recovery and crash-consistency mechanisms, including checkpointing, redo, and undo.

PostgreSQL uses recovery mechanisms to ensure data consistency in the event of a crash or unexpected shutdown. Let's look at each component of recovery and crash-consistency mechanisms in PostgreSQL in detail:

Checkpointing Checkpoints are periodic points in time where PostgreSQL synchronously writes data from memory to disk. This process helps in preventing the accumulation of a lot of changes in memory that could cause a significant delay for recovery operation and crash. Checkpoints allow engines like 'pg_ctl' command to know that they are "caught up" with disk writes by ensuring that the transactions 'commit' before the checkpoint start have been written to disk.

A checkpoint is performed using the 'CHECKPOINT' command. PostgreSQL can also perform auto-checkpoints through its 'checkpoint_timeout' and 'checkpoint_completion_target' configurations.

Redo Redo, also known as Write-ahead logging (WAL), logs changes to the database before alterations are made permanent, a process known as a 'commit'. The log is written to the WAL on the disk, and it is replayed on the system when the engine restarts, which enables the undo process to work even when the page has been flushed.

During database recovery, PostgreSQL replays the WAL to ensure completeness because if it comes across an uncommitted transaction that had been updated in PostgreSQL memory, it writes the values of those changes, which avoids redoing transactions that had already been completed or that crashed the database instance.

To reduce the overhead of redo operations, PostgreSQL can be configured to use background writer paces flushing into the background across group groups. You can also configure the checkpoint and WAL parameters to balance the performance and the recovery time.

Undo The Undo process works hand-in-hand with the Redo process in PostgreSQL. It is responsible for reversing the database's data changes by keeping track of the changes made on the system. In a situation where a database is in recovery mode, and certain transactions haven't been committed, the Undo process is used to ensure that the database maintains consistency.

PostgreSQL's undo mechanism takes the form of transaction IDs. Every transaction has an ID, and with this ID, PostgreSQL knows how to undo the changes made by the transaction. Transactions that didnt commit successfully and those that were started but hadnt completed are undone.

In a scenario where the transaction changes had been written to the disk, the recovery process will take the last successful checkpoint and redo all the changes completed after the checkpoint. Before redoing each item, it checks the transaction ID to verify if the changes were part of a successful transaction to avoid redoing it.

Below is an example of checkpointing implementation in Java:

```java
import java.sql.Connection;
import java.sql.DriverManager;
import java.sql.SQLException;

public class CheckpointExample {

    public static void main(String[] args) throws SQLException {
        String dbName = "mydb";
        String userName = "user";
        String password = "password";
        String url = "jdbc:postgresql://localhost:5432/" + dbName;

        Connection conn = DriverManager.getConnection(url, userName, password);
        conn.createStatement().execute("CHECKPOINT");
        conn.close();
    }
}
```

In this example, we create an instance of a 'Connection' object to PostgreSQL, execute a 'CHECKPOINT', and then close down the connection. This implementation is equivalent to calling 'CHECK-POINT' command in the postgres command line or 'pg_ctl'.

6.15   Discuss the process of developing custom foreign data wrappers (FDWs) for PostgreSQL to integrate with new data sources or APIs.

Foreign Data Wrappers (FDWs) are used in PostgreSQL to integrate external data sources and APIs seamlessly into the database. A custom FDW is a programmatic interface between PostgreSQL and the external data source. Developing a custom FDW requires some technical expertise and knowledge of the PostgreSQL extension API. In this answer, we will discuss the process of developing custom FDWs for PostgreSQL.

1. Determine the External Data Source and its Interface

The first step in developing a custom FDW is to determine the external data source and its interface. The interface defines how data is accessed and manipulated in the external data source. For example, to develop a custom FDW for a web API, a developer needs to understand the APIs endpoints and parameters, the format of data returned by the API and the authentication mechanisms used by the API to secure data access.

2. Plan the External Data Source to PostgreSQL Mapping

The second step is to plan how the external data source will be mapped to PostgreSQL. It is important to understand the data types, data structures and access patterns used by the external data source. The mapping should consider the optimal way to store and access the data in PostgreSQL.

For example, if the external data source returns data in a JSON format, then the developer needs to identify the key-value pairs in the JSON data and map them to PostgreSQL tables and columns. If the external data source returns data in a flat file format, then the developer needs to identify the data fields in the file and map them to PostgreSQL tables and columns.

3. Develop the FDW Code

The third step is to develop the FDW code. There are two parts to the FDW code: the handler code and the wrapper code.

The handler code manages the data access and manipulation operations between PostgreSQL and the external data source. It provides the necessary functions to support SQL statements like SELECT, INSERT, UPDATE, and DELETE. The handler code needs to convert the SQL queries generated by PostgreSQL into the appropriate external data source API calls. For example, for a SELECT query, the handler code needs to fetch the data from the external data source, convert it to the PostgreSQL format, and return it to PostgreSQL.

The wrapper code is the entry point for PostgreSQL to load and unload the FDW. The wrapper code provides the necessary functions to initialize and cleanup the FDW, as well as implementing the Foreign Data Wrapper interface according to the PostgreSQL extension API.

4. Test and Deploy the FDW

The fourth step is to test and deploy the FDW. The developer needs to test the FDW thoroughly to ensure that it works correctly and efficiently. The performance of the FDW should be evaluated, as it can have an impact on the overall performance of PostgreSQL.

Once the FDW has been tested and approved, it can be deployed to integrate the external data source into PostgreSQL. The FDW can be deployed either as a shared library or as a PostgreSQL extension.

Finally, it is important to maintain and update the FDW as necessary. As the external data source or the PostgreSQL version changes, the FDW may need to be updated to ensure continued compatibility and integration.

In summary, developing a custom FDW requires detailed planning, careful consideration of the external data source and its interface, and expertise with the PostgreSQL extension API. By following the steps outlined in this answer, developers can create robust and efficient custom FDWs to integrate external data sources and APIs into PostgreSQL.

6.16 Describe the principles of geographically distributed PostgreSQL deployments, including data replication, consistency, and latency concerns.

Geographically distributed PostgreSQL deployments refer to the setup where one PostgreSQL database is hosted on multiple physical or virtual servers located in different geographic locations. Such deployments are often used for achieving high availability, disaster recovery, and/or better user experience for users located in different parts of the world. The following are some of the key principles and considerations for geographically distributed PostgreSQL deployments:

1. Data Replication: Replication is the process of copying data from one PostgreSQL database (called the primary) to one or more other

PostgreSQL databases (called replicas) located in different geographic locations. Replication can be synchronous or asynchronous. In synchronous replication, the primary waits for confirmation from the replicas that data has been written before confirming the write to the user. Synchronous replication provides stronger consistency guarantees but may introduce more latency. In asynchronous replication, the primary sends data to the replicas without waiting for confirmation. Asynchronous replication may result in some data loss if the primary fails before the data is replicated to the replicas. PostgreSQL supports both synchronous and asynchronous replication, and the choice depends on the specific requirements of the deployment.

2. Consistency: In a geographically distributed deployment, ensuring consistency of data across replicas is important. This can be achieved through the use of strict consistency models such as serializability or snapshot isolation, or through the use of eventual consistency models where data may be temporarily inconsistent but eventually becomes consistent. PostgreSQL supports both strict and eventual consistency models depending on the isolation level set for transactions.

3. Latency: Latency is the time it takes for data to travel between different geographic locations. In a geographically distributed deployment, high latency can lead to performance issues and user dissatisfaction. The choice of replication method and consistency level can significantly affect latency. Synchronous replication introduces more latency than asynchronous replication, while strict consistency models such as serializability may introduce even more latency than eventual consistency models.

4. Load Balancing: In a geographically distributed deployment, load balancing can be used to route user requests to the PostgreSQL database located nearest to the user's location. This can improve user experience and reduce latency. There are several load balancing strategies that can be used, including DNS-based load balancing, round-robin load balancing, and geographic load balancing.

Example Java code for connecting to a geographically distributed PostgreSQL deployment using a JDBC driver:

```
String url = "jdbc:postgresql://<hostname1>,<hostname2>,<hostname3>/<dbname>?
    targetServerType=preferSlave";
Properties props = new Properties();
props.setProperty("user","<username>");
props.setProperty("password","<password>");
```

```
Connection conn = DriverManager.getConnection(url, props);
```

In the above code, '<hostname1>', '<hostname2>', and '<hostname3>' are hostnames or IP addresses of replicas, '<dbname>' is the name of the database, '<username>' and '<password>' are the credentials for connecting to the database. The 'targetServerType=preferSlave' parameter specifies that read queries should be directed to the replica servers rather than the primary server, which can help reduce latency.

6.17 How do you implement real-time analytics and stream processing in PostgreSQL using extensions like TimescaleDB and PipelineDB?

Real-time analytics and stream processing can be implemented in PostgreSQL by using extensions like TimescaleDB and PipelineDB. Both these extensions are designed to process and analyze large volumes of data in real-time. Below are the details on how to implement real-time analytics and stream processing using TimescaleDB and PipelineDB:

1. TimescaleDB:

TimescaleDB is an extension to PostgreSQL that enables real-time analytics and time-series data processing. It is an open-source database that is designed to handle large amounts of data and provide real-time insights into the data. TimescaleDB provides several features that enable real-time analytics and stream processing:

- Hypertables: TimescaleDB uses a hypertable to store time-series data in a PostgreSQL table. This table can be partitioned based on time intervals, making it easy to query and analyze data.

- Continuous Aggregates: TimescaleDB allows you to create continuous aggregates on your time-series data that are automatically updated as new data arrives. This makes it easy to perform real-time analytics on your data.

- Time-Indexed Queries: TimescaleDB provides several time-indexed queries that enable you to query data based on time intervals. These queries are

optimized for time-series data and can be used to perform real-time analytics on data.

Example Code:

Here is an example Java code to connect to the TimescaleDB database
and create a hypertable:

```java
import java.sql.*;

public class TimescaleDBExample {
   public static void main(String args[]) {
      try {
         Class.forName("org.postgresql.Driver");
         String url = "jdbc:postgresql://localhost:5432/mydb";
         String user = "postgres";
         String password = "mypassword";
         Connection conn = DriverManager.getConnection(url, user, password);

         // Create a hypertable
         Statement stmt = conn.createStatement();
         stmt.executeUpdate("CREATE TABLE mytable (time TIMESTAMPTZ NOT NULL,
             data JSONB);");
         stmt.executeUpdate("SELECT create_hypertable('mytable','time');");
         stmt.close();
         conn.close();
      }
      catch(SQLException se) {
         se.printStackTrace();
      }
      catch(Exception e) {
         e.printStackTrace();
      }
   }
}
```

2. PipelineDB:

PipelineDB is an open-source extension to PostgreSQL that enables
real-time stream processing and analytics. It is designed to handle
large volumes of data and provides several features that enable real-
time analytics:

- Continuous Views: PipelineDB allows you to create continuous views
that are automatically updated as new data arrives. These views can be
used to perform real-time analytics on your data.

- Window Functions: PipelineDB provides several window functions that
enable you to perform real-time analytics on your data. These functions
can be used to group and aggregate data based on time periods.

- SQL Interface: PipelineDB provides a SQL interface that enables you
to query your real-time data. This interface is designed to be compatible
with PostgreSQL and allows you to use standard SQL syntax.

Example Code:

Here is an example Java code to connect to the PipelineDB database
and create a continuous view:

```
import java.sql.*;

public class PipelineDBExample {
   public static void main(String args[]) {
      try {
         Class.forName("org.postgresql.Driver");
         String url = "jdbc:postgresql://localhost:5432/mydb";
         String user = "postgres";
         String password = "mypassword";
         Connection conn = DriverManager.getConnection(url, user, password);

         // Create a continuous view
         Statement stmt = conn.createStatement();
         stmt.executeUpdate("CREATE CONTINUOUS VIEW myview AS SELECT AVG(value)
             FROM mytable GROUP BY INTERVAL '1 minute';");
         stmt.close();
         conn.close();
      }
      catch(SQLException se) {
         se.printStackTrace();
      }
      catch(Exception e) {
         e.printStackTrace();
      }
   }
}
```

In conclusion, both TimescaleDB and PipelineDB are powerful extensions to PostgreSQL that enable real-time analytics and stream
processing. They provide several features that make it easy to process and analyze large volumes of data in real-time.

6.18   Discuss the challenges and best prac- tices for migrating large-scale legacy databases to PostgreSQL, including schema conversion, data migration, and performance tuning.

Migrating a large-scale legacy database to PostgreSQL involves several challenges and best practices that need to be considered. In this
answer, I will discuss the major challenges and provide some best
practices on how to overcome them.

Challenges:

1. Schema Conversion: One of the most significant challenges when migrating a database to Postgres is converting the schema. Postgres has some differences in its data types, so you need to review and update your schema before migrating.

2. Data Migration: Since the data in the legacy database is often in a different format than supported in PostgreSQL, data migration becomes a complex task. Additionally, large-scale databases may take a long time to migrate.

3. Performance Tuning: Once you have moved your data to PostgreSQL, you may notice a difference in performance. Postgres has different performance configurations, and you need to optimize it according to your application requirements.

Best Practices:

1. Plan ahead: Migrating a large-scale database to Postgres is a significant undertaking, so it's essential to plan carefully in advance. You can start by analyzing your legacy database, creating a checklist of things that need to be done, and estimating the time and resources required for the migration.

2. Test, Test, Test: Before migrating, test everything - the schema conversion, the data migration, and the queries. It's important to verify that everything is working correctly to avoid any issues post-migration.

3. Use a tool for Data Migration: When it comes to migrating large-scale databases, using an automated tool is the best option. Several third-party tools automate this process, including AWS Database Migration Service, Quest Data Migration Manager, and PostgreSQL's built-in COPY command.

4. Optimize Performance with the right configurations: After migrating the data, you may need to modify the performance of your PostgreSQL database. The correct configuration depends on many factors such as database size, hardware, and query load. Ensure that you analyze your data and tweak the PostgreSQL parameters to your application's requirements.

5. Create a Rollback Plan: Finally, before migrating, ensure that you have a rollback plan in case something goes wrong. It is essential to have a plan in place to migrate back to your existing database, which requires ensuring you retain backups of both the legacy database and PostgreSQL database.

Overall, with careful planning and execution, it is possible to migrate large-scale legacy databases to PostgreSQL successfully. Test and re-test the schema conversion, data migration, and queries to ensure everything is working correctly. With proper performance tuning, you should see your PostgreSQL database's performance improve compared to your legacy database.

6.19   Explain the internals of PostgreSQL's memory management and caching mechanisms, such as the buffer cache, shared buffers, and local caches.

PostgreSQL's memory management and caching mechanisms are crucial to its performance and scalability. The system incorporates several aspects of memory management, including the buffer cache, shared buffers, and local caches.

The buffer cache is the first layer of caching in PostgreSQL, which stores blocks of data read from the disk. It is managed by the operating system and is shared among all processes that access the disk. The buffer cache provides a way to reduce the number of I/O operations by serving as a temporary storage for blocks that have recently been read. When a request for a block is made, PostgreSQL checks the buffer cache for the requested block before reading from disk.

The next layer of caching is the shared buffer pool. This is an area of memory that is dedicated to caching frequently accessed data from the buffer cache. It is managed by PostgreSQL and is shared among all backends (database connections). The main purpose of the shared buffer pool is to reduce the number of disk reads required to satisfy database queries. When a backend requests a block of data, PostgreSQL checks the shared buffer pool for the requested block. If the block is found, it is returned immediately. If the block is not found, PostgreSQL reads it from the buffer cache and adds it to the shared buffer pool for future use.

In addition to the shared buffer pool, PostgreSQL also has local caches. Local caches are used to cache data that is specific to a single backend or query. They are intended to be used for frequently executed queries that require a small amount of data. Local caches are implemented as memory context's with the configuration option memory_context_enable set to on. For example, you could use a local cache to cache the results of an often-executed query by using a hash table or similar data structure to store the results in memory.

PostgreSQL manages memory using its own memory allocator, which is optimized for the allocation patterns commonly used by the database server. The memory allocator allocates memory from the operating system in large blocks, and then subdivides those blocks into smaller chunks that can be used for individual database objects. It is designed to avoid the overheads associated with traditional memory management systems, such as fragmentation and lock contention.

Overall, PostgreSQL's memory management and caching mechanisms are highly optimized for performance and scalability. By utilizing the buffer cache, shared buffer pool, and local caches, PostgreSQL is able to reduce the number of expensive disk reads and provide high levels of concurrency for multiple database connections.

6.20   Describe the process of diagnosing and resolving issues related to data corruption, disk failures, and hardware faults in a PostgreSQL environment.

Diagnosing and resolving issues related to data corruption, disk failures, and hardware faults in a PostgreSQL environment can be a complex process, but there are steps that can be taken to help identify the root cause of the problem and take necessary actions to fix it.

1. Identify the Symptoms: First and foremost, identify the symptoms of the issue. The symptoms may range from sluggish database performance to complete system failure. Knowing the symptoms can aid in zeroing in on the root cause.

2. Diagnose the issue: Once symptoms have been identified, it is essential to diagnose the issue. PostgreSQL has several diagnostic tools, including the PostgreSQL log files. These logs often contain error messages and other critical information regarding database performance. To diagnose the issue, it is always better to begin by examining the logs.

3. Database Corruption: If the logs point to database corruption, it is essential not to panic. PostgreSQL has several tools to fix database corruption, including pg_resetxlog and pg_resetwal. These commands can assist in resetting the database to a clean state, and may recover lost data.

4. Disk Failures: Disk failures are another potential cause of database issues in PostgreSQL. If you suspect this, the system administrator should use the appropriate tool to inspect the disks. SMART monitoring tools can help identify disk failures or other issues that may cause disk problems.

5. Hardware Faults: Hardware faults are typically caused by either hardware failures or hardware inconsistencies. Hardware inconsistencies due to failing or inconsistent power sources, memory errors, network card failures are some examples of possible hardware faults that can cause database corruption. Physical inspection, server logs, and system stress tests can identify these types of hardware issues.

6. Resolve the issue: Once the root cause of the issue is identified, it's time to resolve it. If database corruption is detected, restoring from a recent backup may help resolve the issue. Hardware failures may require necessary component replacement, and hardware inconsistencies may require system upgrades, including the installation of a UPS.

7. Perform post-resolution checks: After the issue is resolved, it is important to perform essential checks to ensure that the database is running smoothly. System administrators should check logs, run system stress tests, and review backup scripts to prevent further data

corruption.

In summary, Diagnosing and resolving issues related to data corruption, disk failures, and hardware faults in a PostgreSQL environment requires a proper understanding of PostgreSQL databases, diagnostic tools, and hardware components. Following the outlined steps, from identifying symptoms through to performing post-resolution checks, can help increase the likelihood of a successful resolution.

www.ingramcontent.com/pod-product-compliance
Lightning Source LLC
LaVergne TN
LVHW051334050326
832903LV00031B/3527